The covers collected [in these volumes] show exactly what covers are designed to do – stimulate eye and mind – and also act with Pavlovian intensity on the designer/reader's behaviour knowingly or not. They are indeed meant to have IMPACT.

Steven Heller

Impact 2.0
—
Design magazines, journals
and periodicals [1974–2016]

Unit 28

Contents

Foreword
—
The editors

This book and its companion volume, *Impact 1.0, Design magazines, journals and periodicals [1922–73]*, have their origins in two visits made by Tony Brook. The first was to the University of the Creative Arts (UCA) archive in Epsom, UK, and the second was to the Herb Lubalin Study Center of Design and Typography in New York, USA. Both locations house a superabundance of design magazines from the early 20th century to the present day. The opportunity to make a book out of these stellar collections was too good to pass up.

At its core, these volume are an attempt to catalogue the excellence of design magazines, journals and periodicals catering for design of all kinds. We've chosen to only show covers – and only covers that exhibit superior design values. Interestingly, this means that the publications we have included here also tend to be the publications that have the most merit. Poor covers usually mean poor content.

We have spread our net wide. Although the covers shown here are mostly from graphic design publications, we have included some from architecture and material design – but again, only when the design is exemplary.

These are also books that seek to acknowledge the contribution that the editors, writers, publishers and designers of journals have made to the evolution of design. Without the design press, we are entitled to wonder if design would have travelled quite so rapidly from a marginal artisanal craft of the industrial era to the sophisticated communication and information discipline that it is in today's information era.

We take them for granted, we even allow them to wither away, but a discipline without its journals of record is hard to conceive.

The Language of Design Magazine Covers
—
Steven Heller

Originally coined in the early 1920s, the term *graphic design* represented a category straddling what was then called decorative arts and mass communications. It signified the practice of printing typefaces and imagery on physical materials, notably paper, wherein aesthetics rather than purely function took precedence. If you could talk with any of the graphic design masters, like AM Cassandre, Paul Rand or WA Dwiggins, who first used the term as a way to more precisely distinguish printers and compositors from commercial artist/designers, they'd tell you that the term has gone through various transitions and manifestations. The current digital age is in one of those transitional periods.

Of course, talking to long deceased masters about design is impossible. But if you are resourceful there exists an accessible way whereby questions about the origins and evolution of graphic design can be answered. And, by the way, you are holding it in your hands right now.

Most of the essential ideas, key texts and iconic images are available for all to see in a genre of specialised design magazines and journals where pioneers and visionaries were interviewed, showcased or wrote articles themselves. For those who study design history, this critical mass of design magazines are part Dead Sea Scrolls and part Rosetta Stone. Yet only recently have they been taken as seriously. Some have been digitised and open-sourced, while many others are only analog. Which is a pity, really. Since there were hundreds of different ink-on-paper trade and lifestyle magazines, scholarly journals and promotional periodicals published over the past hundred-plus-years, which are arguably the best historical resources at our disposal, short of digging through raw material, job-bags, letters and notes in assorted personal archives and institutional libraries.

Even early trade magazines published before the modern era hold treasures that speak volumes about our legacy. During the late 19th and early 20th centuries, most of these publications addressed graphic design as an offshoot of the printing and typographic industries. Printers employed compositors to set and compose type (which had quantifiable retail value) while design was thrown in as an extra part of the job. Trade magazines with the names *The American Printer* (1883–2011, USA), *The Inland Printer* (1883–1941, USA), *The American Model Printer* (1879–unknown, USA) – you get the idea – started including sections on typesetting, type founding and eventually type styling and typography. Since typography had become the tool of advertising, which developed into an industry during the era of commercial erchandising, advertising trade journals were founded that emphasised the best ways to use type and layout, which, by any other name, was graphic design.

During the last quarter of the nineteenth century, specialised professional periodicals began to appear that were devoted to everything from showcasing printing press and foundry hardware to introducing typefaces to celebrating poster artists to following graphic styles and movements. As the printing and graphics trades further matured and the commercial arts expanded, magazines that reported, critiqued and even argued about the emerging advertising design profession insured the legitimacy of the field on many levels, not the least of which were setting standards and best practices.

Having rummaged through a fair number of dead and living designers' attics and basements, I can report one truth: most designers have held onto their favourite design magazines for as long as possible on the off-chance that they might need to reference them some day. Since they are considered valuable artifacts, when the time finally comes to discard them – as it does to every aging or transient designer – these magazines are rarely junked. Instead, they are sold, donated or handed down to younger designers as if they were tablets from the mount. Which means that a lot of the important magazines get transferred from one library or archive to another, an act of content preservation that benefits everyone who cares about design history – which should be every designer.

Design magazines are our Lascaux caves, *Encyclopedia Britannica* and *True Confessions* rolled between covers. Or if that analogy seems strained,

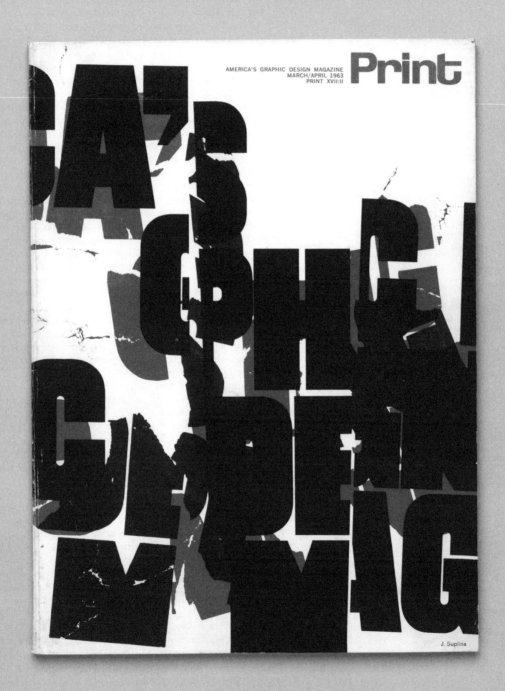

AMERICA'S GRAPHIC DESIGN MAGAZINE
MARCH/APRIL 1963
PRINT XVII:II

Print

J. Suplina

Print
Country: USA   Cover Design: Joseph Suplina

consider them as snapshots of the profession from its beginnings to now. Fortunately for historians, a substantially large percentage of these magazines had extremely long durations – *Print* (1940–present, USA), magazine, for instance, just celebrated 75 years of continuous publishing, a span that makes it the most historically valuable of them all. Others with runs beyond twenty years include the Japanese *IDEA* (1953–present, Japan), *Eye* (1990–present, UK), and *CA* (*Communication Arts*) (1959–present, USA). But even the antiques, like the German *Das Plakat* (1910–21), or French *Arts & Metiers Graphiques* (1927–39), which long ago discontinued publishing, are historically invaluable for how and what they covered during their respective ages in real time. More recent folded journals are just as important. Without *Emigre* (1984–2005, USA), for example, the early computer years that triggered the legibility wars would be lost in the miasma of time; without *U&lc* (1970–99, USA) the transitory period between the introduction of phototype and emergence of digital would not be well chronicled. Even the short-lived publications, like *Neue Grafik* (1958–65, Switzerland), and *Dot Zero* (1966–68, USA) among many others, highlight different important aspects of the mid-century Modernist ideas of 'rightness of form'.

Vintage and contemporary magazines provide vivid viewpoints of fashions, styles, philosophies, trends, evolutions, revolutions, and just about anything that adds substance to our overarching design knowledge. Reading original articles, essays and interviews are revelatory links to the distant and recent past. Even for those who don't care a whit about design history, design magazines are founts of practical inspiration – like virtual mentors. And even if the inside content fails to give contemporary designers enough inspirational raw meat, design magazine covers not only reflect their respective times but quite a few either started or perpetuated trends that were mimicked and became popular.

Design magazine covers are *tabulae rasae*, where artists and designers are given – no, commanded to take – license in order to experiment anew or build upon existing visions. Designers have regularly used design magazine covers to try out ideas that could never be produced for commercial magazines, but nonetheless often influenced them later.

It has been the design magazine cover's role to not only inform their readers – mostly art directors and designers – but even more important, to sanction new developments and encourage greater widespread application of them. I've heard dozens of times from innovative designers that their own inspirations came from the magazines they read. Rand learned about the Bauhaus from imports like the British *Commercial Art* (1922–1959) magazine and the German *Gebrauchsgraphik* (1923–50, Germany), just like the Beatles learned rock and roll from imported American records.

Of course, there was a chicken-and-egg paradox. Design magazines are not always engines of change. Most of them mirrored what was already in the works or in the air, rather than serve as avant garde revolutionaries. Moreover, even design magazines did not always offer its cover designers unfettered freedom to start from scratch. Most are inflexible, especially when it comes to things like their logo or nameplate's look and size. While many covers, including the original *Gebrauchsgraphik* edited by FK Frenzel and Swiss *Graphis* (1944–present, Switzerland), edited by Walter Herdeg, allowed designers to incorporate custom logos into their design, rigidity also held sway from time to time.

Still, most of the covers shown here attest that limits were (and are) less restrictive (and the results more surprising) than most publishing venues. After all, design magazine covers must be unconventional and inspirational, or what's the point? A truly memorable design cover is a little – or a lot – like designer pin-ups (and design porno).

Being showcased on a design magazine cover is, therefore, a major coup on various levels – at least for those magazines that regularly commission different artists and designers. First is credibility: for the lucky cover artist receiving that prize has far reaching ramifications. Second is opportunity: this is a great chance for a designer to make a bold statement. Third is notoriety:

Idea
1953—present
Japan

Neue Grafik
1958—65
Switzerland

Graphis
1944—present
Switzerland

the cover designer will be in the public's eyes and on the lips of her peers. Careers are born on covers.

But as this book attests, not all covers are customised one-offs. (*Das*) *Werk* (1914–present, Switzerland), *ulm* (1958–68, Germany), *Neue Grafik* and others were credible and authoritative precisely because they stayed true to an inviolable format that transmitted rationality and purity in an otherwise eclectic environment. Most of all, a cover design should telegraph the unique character and personality of the magazine it is covering. *Graphis*, like *Print* and others, was always a window onto a featured artist inside. The Swiss *Typographische Monatsblätter* (1932–present, Switzerland) routinely projected new developments in typographic rationality. *Typographica* (1949–67, UK) projected the marriage of tradition and the avant garde. In each case the decision about which cover to publish carried considerable weight.

The covers collected for this incredible volume show exactly what covers are designed to do – stimulate eye and mind, but also to act with Pavlovian intensity on the designer/reader's behavior, knowingly or not. They are indeed meant to have IMPACT. And as we head deeper into the age of hand-held devices and responsive screens, where magazines like the ones here turn into online experiences, these great covers will become obsolete. So, it is for this reason that preserving and archiving these documents of international design, one cover at a time, is beyond useful, it is imperative in tracing the evolution of design and the importance of designers in our culture. There is a certain magic in these covers that triggers better work in all design makers. Or to paraphrase Ray Bradbury in *Fahrenheit 431*: the magic is not only in what covers say, its 'how they stitched the patches of the universe together into one garment for us.'

(Das) Werk
1914—present
Switzerland

TM
1932—present
Switzerland

Typographica
1949—67
UK

010

ulm 8/9

Zeitschrift der Hochschule für Gestaltung   Journal of the Hochschule für Gestaltung

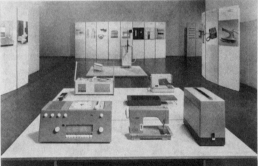

VISIBLE LANGUAGE

Volume VIII
Number 2 Spring 1974

The Journal for Research
on the Visual Media
of Language Expression

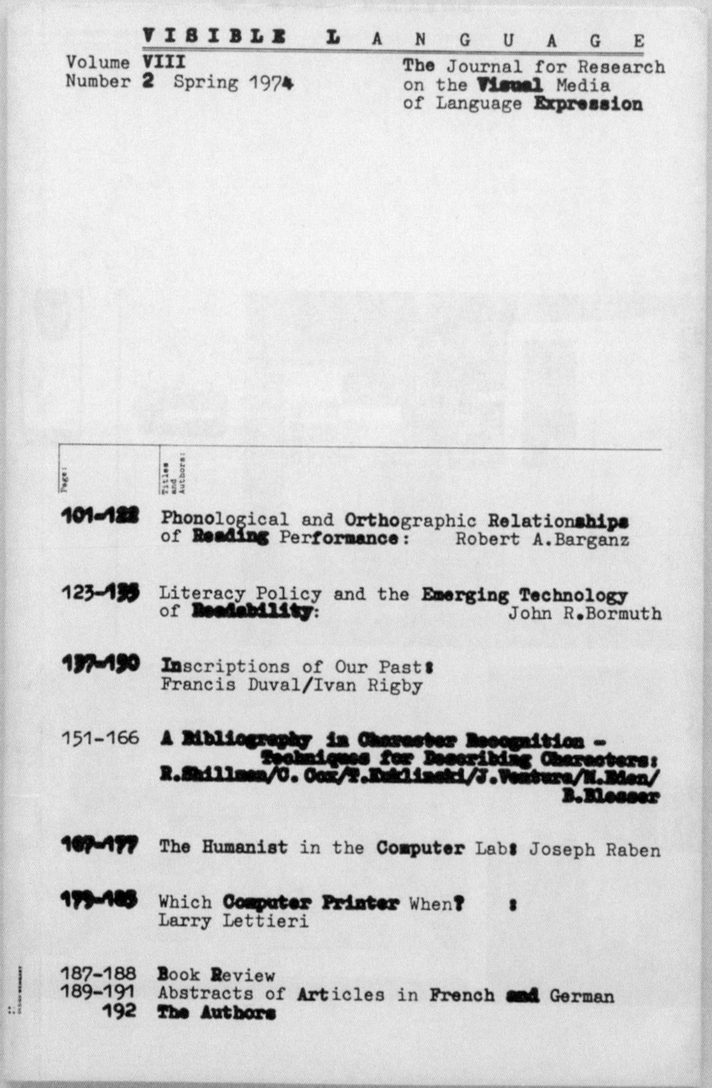

Visible Language
Country: USA

Cover Design: Wolfgang Weingart

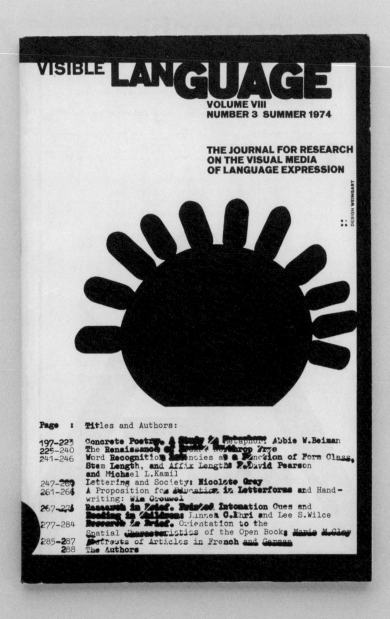

A quarterly Review of International
Visual Communication Design

icographic

7

Issue number 7, 1974

Price per issue 1 US dollar

Published in London by the
International Council of Graphic
Design Associations

Contents include

Type in our environment
A proposition for education in
letterforms and handwriting

Investigation into colour preferences
Swiss posters for Amnesty
International
Signposting and communication
media

Concerning signposting
Sound-writing
Typographical training for
technicians and technical
training for typographers

Patrick Wallis Burke

Icographic
Country: UK

Cover Design: Patrick Wallis Burke

Zeitschrift für verbale und visuelle Kommunikation   10. Jg. Heft 4   Juli 74   P 20638 F

50 ›Format›

Format
Country: Germany

Cover Design:
Manfred Glemser & Gret Lengerer

A quarterly Review of International
Visual Communication Design

Issue number 8, 1974

icographic

8

Price per issue 1.5 US dollars

Published in London by the
International Council of Graphic
Design Associations

Contents include

One writing for one world—
the pioneer work of C K Bliss
TyposAsia 74

Stamp on it—some aspects of
postage stamp design
Communication in an environment
and by an environment
The roots of the problem

Easier than ABC—some experiments
with a 'plastic' language
Six thousand years of writing
How to design in Chinese (without
really being able to read it)

Henry Steiner

Icographic
Country: UK

Cover Design: Yeung Wai-fung,
Patrick Wallis Burke

AaBbCcDdEeFfGgHhIiJjKkLlMmNnOoPp   QqRrSsTtUuVvWwXxYyZz1234567890&ÆŒ$¢£%!?()[]

UPPER AND LOWER CASE, THE INTERNATIONAL JOURNAL OF TYPOGRAPHICS   PUBLISHED BY THE INTERNATIONAL TYPEFACE CORPORATION, VOLUME TWO, NUMBER FOUR 1975

In This Issue:

ITC Competition
The results are in from our first annual Upper and Lower Case International Typographics Competition—initiated to attract examples of typographic excellence in which ITC typefaces were utilized.

Copyrights, Typefaces & You
Congress is now considering a major revision of the copyright law. The editorial explores the new ethical climate it will bring should such a bill become law and exactly what it would mean to the world of typefaces and to you.

Happy Holidays 1976
"Silence is the fittest reply to folly." This ancient Arabic proverb has nothing whatever to do with the above title—being nothing more than a brazen diversion to cover our late appearance with the season's greetings.

Deidi's Walls
Deidi Von Schaewen is a talented graphic designer/photographer whose dazzling photographic display of exceptional walls are soon to be seen the world over in her forthcoming book.

Ms. Susie and Dorothy Yule
According to Webster, yule is an exclamation expressive of joy at Christmastime; according to U&lc, it's the surname of identical twin sisters whose artistry brings joy the year round.

A Christmas Feast
Now who in the world would think of contributing an article to this publication of a 3-colored Italian Christmas feast—in glorious black and white? Mo Lebowitz, that's who! For a delicious sampling of his unique wit, we heartily recommend that you put on your bib, get out your Pantone book, and join us in a delightful Lebowitz Christmas feast.

Ampersands
Last issue, we introduced a new feature of famous ampersands, illustrated with commentary by Jerome Snyder. The man's extension of a good idea seems virtually limitless—so here again, eight additional fantastic ampersands.

Something from Everybody for U&lc
We really started something when we casually suggested that those who liked us (and those who didn't) might drop us a line or two if it pleased them. Well, we asked for it and we got it—with illustrations thrown in for good measure.

Something for Everybody from U&lc
A regular feature of titillating trivia that also conveys practical knowledge, cements arguments, comments on the oddities of life, and demonstrates (sometimes) universal truths.

French Postcards
If you're thinking the above is a put-on, and we're only going to con you with vicarious thoughts of Montmartre, you're wrong. So let your sexual fantasies run amok, skip quickly past the earlier pages, and—oh well, let Herb Lubalin tell you all about it. He was there.

What's New From ITC?
ITC Bookman in four weights (Light, Medium, Demi, and Bold) are the new typefaces from ITC which licensed subscribers are authorized to reproduce, manufacture, and offer for sale.

Crossword Puzzle
Gertrude Snyder, like her spouse Jerome, has a very fertile mind. In this instance, she's turned it to a crossword puzzle—but with an added catch. Whether or not you're a crossword freak, we think you'll find Gertrude's puzzle a real typographic challenge.

PAGE 1

PAGE 8

PAGE 10

PAGE 16

PAGE 20

PAGE 28

PAGE 36

PRESENTING THE WINNERS OF THE FIRST ANNUAL UPPER & LOWER CASE INTERNATIONAL TYPOGRAPHICS COMPETITION

We are pleased to report that our first annual competition—initiated to attract examples of typographic excellence in which ITC typefaces were utilized—has met with a reader response far exceeding even the outside hopes of our editors.

More than 1000 entries were submitted, with a gratifyingly high number of pieces superior in quality and imagination.

Although Price, Waterhouse wasn't engaged, in this instance, to vouch for the sanctity of the sealed envelope containing names of the winners, no other stone was left unturned by the U&lc staff to insure a competition that would be at once without favoritism and completely above reproach.

The jury, which judged each and every entry, reads like a virtual "Who's Who" in the graphics design field. The jurors were such prominent leaders in the field as Lou Dorfsman, Ruth Ansel, Gene Federico, Milton Glaser, Gennaro Andreozzi, and George Lois.

CONTINUED ON PAGE 3

Country: USA

Cover Design: Lubalin, Smith, Carnase & Peckolick

017

Idea
Country: Japan

Cover Design: Hiroshi Ohchi

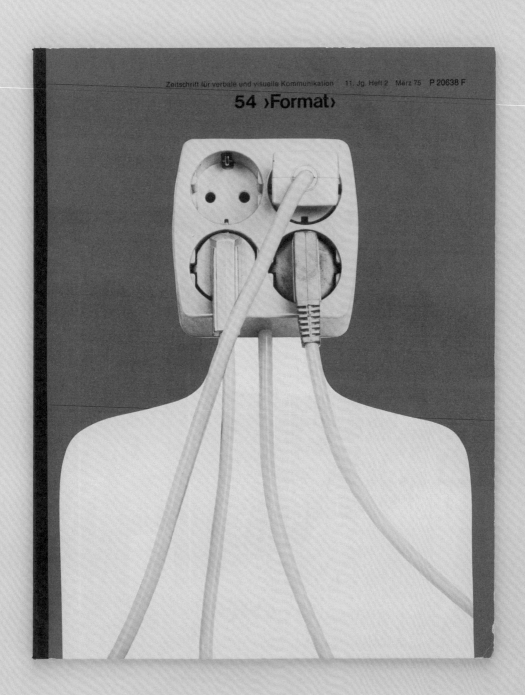

Zeitschrift für verbale und visuelle Kommunikation 11. Jg. Heft 2 März 75 P 20638 F

54 ›Format›

Format
Country: Germany   Cover Design: Schott GmbH

AR (The Architectural Review)
Country: UK

Cover Painting: Ben Johnson

Q What do you look for in an architectural magazine/journal?

A A few dichotomous things. Speed and depth: the ability to read it in seconds, or the invitation to read it in depth. These tend to be, for me, mutually exclusive. If I am looking for a quick read, it is rare for me to return to the magazine for longer articles. Are they books or are they flashcards? Both work for different reasons, at different times.

Focus and range: either a very narrow focus on a specific topic, aspect, phenomenon, designer, idea, or a breadth that goes beyond architecture. Someone quoted me recently as saying 'being better at architecture means doing more than architecture', which is rather clever even if I don't remember saying it! I'm interested in either near-limitless depth, or a range that extends far beyond just architecture.

Pictures and words: we live and work in a visual world, and sometimes all we want or need are images. They may not provide a full backstory, but when one visits a building (corporeally or virtually) there is rarely a narration explaining the architect's ideas. As teachers we always tell students, 'but you won't be there to explain that'. But words matter and real text, with or without images, provides the connecting tissue that purely visual ideas don't.

Q What were the first American architectural magazines that caught your attention?

A *Progressive Architecture* (1945–95, USA) was the bible when I was in school and early practice. UK mags were more interesting: *AD* (1930–present) and *Architectural Review* (1896–present) were both great (*AD* was at one point edited by Theo Crosby, later my partner at Pentagram, with Monica Pidgeon), as were *Blueprint* (1983–present) and *Wallpaper** (1996–present) later. Journals like Yale University's *Perspecta* (1952–present, USA) and similar ones from Penn and Harvard were the intellectual's choice. And *Oppositions* (1973–84, USA) was the smart journal from the Institute for Architecture and Urban Studies. Plus, Massimo Vignelli designed it! *El Croquis* (1982–present, Spain), *A+U* (1971–present, Japan) and similar special, mostly monographic, journals are the 'fast books' of the industry. And of course there was, and is, *Domus* (1928–present, Italy) and *Lotus* (1963–present, Italy) and *Casabella* (1928–present, Italy) and *Ottagono* (1966–present, Italy) and...

Q Which journals offer the best content for contemporary practising architects?

A Almost anything but the standards. And there are many newspaper journalists (Michael Kimmelman, Alice Rawsthorn, Deyan Sudjic) offering thoughtful perspectives on architecture. Plus *Log* (2003–present, USA), *Clog* (2011–present, USA), *Uncube* (2012–present, Germany), *Cultured* (2010–present, USA), act more like periodical books than magazines. And that doesn't even crack the blog world. Finally there is Twitter and other snippets for the attention-challenged, and Instagram for the visually-inclined.

Q How would you categorise the state of architectural journalism today, bearing in mind the dominance of the Internet as an unregulated space for commentary and critique?

A There is now a fine-grained gradation of architecture journalism, online and in print, ranging from the daily reports issued by *The Architect's Newspaper* (2002–present, USA), *Architizer* (2009–present, USA), *ArchDaily* (2008–present, USA), to the weekly summaries of *Fast Company* (1995–present, USA), *CLAD* (2015–present, UK), *Azure* (1985–present, Canada), *Dezeen* (2006–present, UK), to more permanent weekly, monthly and quarterly print reviews. Most publications profess medium agnosticism and will take your attention no matter how they get it.

While I was once all about paper (even going as far as memorialising my books in our glass 'Book Cube') I admit that I read *The New York Times* (1851–present, USA) almost exclusively online (though it is also delivered in paper) and the same is true for architecture publications. Without consciously collecting them I now have screens from iPhone to iPad mini, to iPad Pro to laptops and desktop machines. Five different sizes, each in vivid colour.

AR
1896—present
UK

AR
1896—present
UK

And aggregators like Apple News have become my shortcut to everything I want to skim.

At some point in the 1980s architecture became fashionable and was expected to move at the speed of fashion. Publications have finally caught up. And while it is easy to say that the short form has shortened thinking, and that computers have replaced hand-eye drawing coordination, architecture is better than ever. It is more interesting than ever, more discussed than I can remember and more relevant than it has been in decades. Publications are in large part responsible for this. Most architecture is seen by people in images, not live and in person, and publications of every medium are where we all find those images.

James Biber is a New York-based architect, and was the first architect partner at Pentagram New York. In 2010 he set up his own 'design-led architect firm', and works include the Harley-Davidson Museum, and the Visitor Center for Philip Johnson's Glass House.

**Blueprint
1983—present
UK**

**Casabella
1928—present
Italy**

Graphic Design
Country: Japan

Cover Design: Fukuda Shigeo

PIANO & ROGERS
AT Directory Part 3

ARCHITECTURAL DESIGN VOLUME XLV MAY 1975

AD (Architectural Design)
Country: UK
Design: unidentified

De tweede vorm, mei 1975
maandblad voor vormgeving

Uitgave: Stichting
Industriële Vormgeving

DE 2E
vorm

JURIAAN SCHROFER METRO

Langzamerhand zijn velen gaan begrijpen dat de (Amsterdamse) Metro er niet moet komen. De architecten Aldo van Eyck en Theo Bosch zijn zich gaan afvragen: 'Waar zijn wij als architecten in hemelsnaam mee bezig? We werken meer aan negatieve maatschappelijke processen'. Waar zijn we mee bezig, is een vraag, die ook in de Werkgroep Metro (die o.a. adviseert over de aankoop van kunst voor de metro) gesteld is. Jurriaan Schrofer zit in die werkgroep en verwoordt 't een en ander; hij wordt misselijk als hij ziet wat er gebeurt maar vindt dat 'eruit stappen ook niet de oplossing is van het probleem'.
Pag. 6

THEATER SYSTEEM

'In de praktijk komt het erop neer dat er theaters worden neergezet die misschien wel fraai zijn, maar toch niet meer dan om gestroomlijnde uitgave van de 19e eeuwse schouwburg. Opdrachtgever noch architect laten zich veel gelegen liggen aan de eisen die het snel veranderende toneel stelt'. Dat zei Ritsaert ten Cate van Mickery eens. Zijn theater in Amsterdam is het bewijs dat 't best anders kan.
Het theatermeubilair heeft onder de naam Mickery Module wereldfaam gekregen.
Zie pag. 4 en 5

VREDESDUIVEN, REGENBOGEN SWASTIKA'S

Dertig jaar na het einde van de tweede wereldoorlog vormen affiches 'een waardige herinnering aan de historische overwinning op de nazies'. De bewuste affiches werden ontworpen naar aanleiding van een door de Polen uitgeschreven wedstrijd. Wim Crouwel zat in de jury en zag vooral vredesduiven, regenbogen en swastika's, maar daarnaast ook nog wel iets oorspronkelijkers.
Zie pag. 3

PLAGIAAT, ROOF OF VLEIERIJ

Sommigen zien in namaak de hoogste vorm van vleierij. Anderen houden 't bij diefstal. Plagiaat in de industriële vormgeving en de bescherming ertegen staan centraal in een tentoonstelling in het Stedelijk museum en tijdens een symposium en een studiedag.
De nieuwe Beneluxwet inzake tekeningen en modellen krijgt daar natuurlijk veel aandacht.
Zie o.m. pag. 11

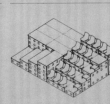

De derde vorm, juni/juli 1975
maandblad voor vormgeving

Uitgave: Stichting
Industriële Vormgeving

DE 3E vorm

DE VORM

De Vorm, een blad dat in controlled circulations wordt verspreid. Wat daarbij een vereiste is, dat is een handtekening van de lezers onder een verklaring dat zij het blad inderdaad willen lezen. Zie hierover ook pag. 2. En zie de antwoordkaart, die moet worden ingevuld en geretourneerd.

DE APPEL

De Stichting De Appel begon in april van dit jaar om een confrontatie tot stand te brengen van het publiek met speciaal van dat deel van de beeldende kunst dat zich toelegt op het maken en tonen van environments, situatiekunst en performances. Ofwel: intermedia. Daarover, en over het pakhuis dat voor De Appel werd verbouwd, enkele impressies op pag. 15

JANTJE WEGWEZEN

Een waar verhaal over twee tandartsen en een interieur-architect, die met z'n drieën een vrijwel optimale werkomgeving hebben gecreëerd voor de tandartsengroepspraktijk van de eerste twee. Een praktijkcentrum dat mede gericht is op een plezieriger verhouding tussen tandarts en patiënt dan helaas in ons land nog meestal wordt aangetroffen. "We hopen dat deze omgeving ons in staat stelt werkelijke tandheelkunde te bedrijven. Optimaal sociaal-medisch te functioneren". Het ziet er naar uit dat het experiment gaat lukken ook. Zie pag. 11

PIET ZWART 90 JAAR

THEORIE EN PRAKTIJK

In Delft werd een dag gepraat over bewegwijzering, in Amsterdam over plagiaat in de industriële vormgeving. Beide studiebijeenkomsten omvatten sterk theoretische beschouwingen naast overzichten van vooral in de praktijk vergaarde inzichten. En beide studiebijeenkomsten krijgen een vervolg: resp. in een permanent interdisciplinair overleg en in een plagiaat-collectie. Zie pag. 7 en pag 10

RIETVELD SCHRÖDERHUIS

Aan het Utrechtse Schröder Huis zijn de opvattingen van Gerrit Rietveld ten aanzien van architectuur en vormgeving het beste af te lezen. In elke Rietveld-studie is het hoofdstuk dat dit huis behandelt dan ook het langst. En terecht. Het is minder terecht dat de rol die mevrouw Tr. Schröder-Schräder in het ontstaansproces heeft gespeeld dikwijls wordt verontachtzaamd. Dankzij háár maakte Rietveld zijn meest uitgesproken werkstuk. Zie pag. 3.

Zeitschrift für verbale und visuelle Kommunikation   11. Jg. Heft 4   Juli 75   P 20638 F

56 ›Format‹

Format
Country: Germany

Cover Design:
Graphic-Design Manz

icographic

9

A biennial Review of International
Visual Communication Design

Issue number 9

Price per issue 1.5 US Dollars

Published in London by the
International Council of Graphic
Design Associations

Contents include

Edugraphology—the myths of design
and the design of myths
World language without words

The myth of the 26 letter Roman
alphabet
Sound-Spell, an alphabet and
a policy
The book in a TV-age

Soundspel—an American approach
to a phonetic alphabet
Two approaches to book cover design
Kingsley Read—a pioneer worker for
an English phonetic alphabet

Patrick Wallis Burke

Icographic
Country: UK

Cover Design: Yeung Wai-fung,
Patrick Wallis Burke

THE ARCHITECTURAL REVIEW PREVIEW VOLUME CLIX NUMBER 947 JANUARY 1976 75p

AR (The Architectural Review)
Country: UK

Cover Design: Philip Thompson

AR (The Architectural Review)
Country: UK
Design: unidentified

U&lc.

Aa Bb Cc Dd Ee Ff Gg Hh Ii Jj Kk Ll Mm Nn Oo Pp   Qq Rr Ss Tt Uu Vv Ww Xx Yy Zz 1234567890 & ÆŒ $¢ £%!?()[]

UPPER AND LOWER CASE, THE INTERNATIONAL JOURNAL OF TYPOGRAPHICS   PUBLISHED BY INTERNATIONAL TYPEFACE CORPORATION, VOLUME THREE, NUMBER TWO, JULY 1976

The Sad State of the Union
A satirical comment by Geoffrey Moss on our highly revered American way of life, our institutions, our systems, and the folks in charge. **Pg 2**

The Publick Printer
The first in a new series by **U&lc** tracing the remarkable history of printing in America beginning, naturally enough, with the beginnings. **Pg 6**

U&lc's Presidential "Primary"
Handsomely-engraved portraits of each of our 37 presidents, taken from the Ralph Ginzburg Collection, wherein we are inviting our readers to select their primary choice of the one president they believe would be most suited to lift the country out of its doldrums. **Pg 8**

Sam Fink's Typographic Paintings
Whoever said there was nothing new under the sun obviously hadn't seen the art of Sam Fink. Blending words and illustrations is a highly specialized skill, as evidenced from the stunning examples within. **Pg 14**

The Fifty-Six Who Signed
Sam Fink seems to have a monopoly on this issue, but he's worth it. This time around, he shows us his uncanny perceptive portrait of all the signers of the Declaration of Independence, with an incisive profile of each. **Pg 18**

Erté: The Artist and his Coterie of Female Characters
Four pages in full color of the famed Alphabet and Numerals of America's foremost fashion illustrator. **Pg 18**

Our Bicentennial Turkey
Following a lengthy discussion with Ben Franklin, Vikki Romaine—designer of toys for adults—has created, especially for this issue, a new symbol for America. **Pg 22**

What's New from ITC?
Under special license from D. Stempel AG, ITC offers a redesigned and smartly updated version of Rudolph Koch's original Kabel, created in the early 1920s and now available from ITC Subscribers as ITC Kabel. **Pg 24**

Someone for Everybody
The space, customarily devoted to our regular features "Something for Everybody" and "Famous Ampersands" is devoted instead to Jerome Snyder, whose death was such an unexpected shock to everyone who knew him and such a severe loss to us all. **Pg 26**

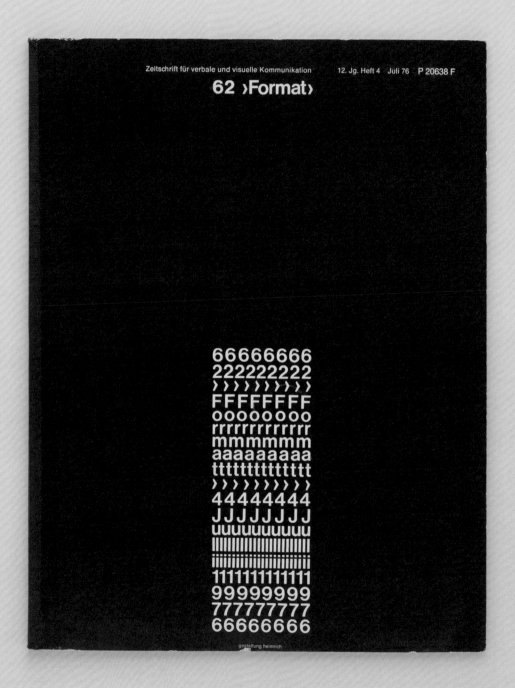

Format
Country: Germany
Design: unidentified

Cover Design: Patrick Wallis Burke

12 1976	Typografische Monatsblätter	Schweizer Grafische Mitteilungen	Revue suisse de l'Imprimerie Edition spéciale Décembre 1976
TM		SGM	RSI

Eine Auswahl **bestimmter Arbeiten** Weingarts von 1969 bis 1976. Gedanken und Beobachtungen eines Freundes. Und persönliche Bemerkungen von ihm.

Ist diese Typografie noch zu retten?

Oder leben wir auf dem Mond? Is This Typography Worth Supporting, Or Do We Live On The Moon? A special selection from the works of Weingart. from 1969-1976. Thoughts and observations of a friend. And personal comments from the author.

0001
0094
Die Typografie ist noch nicht tot! Sie wirkt zwar heute ein bisschen Typography is not dead, yet! But its effect is undoubtedly **blutarm und unentschlossen. Doch im grossen und ganzen ist sie in Ordnung.** anemic and vague. But by and large, it is intact. It is definitely less than ever

0002
0095
Sie ist zwar weniger denn je eine Gebrauchskunst. Dafür aber steht ihr a practical skill. Instead, it endures as an intrinsic necessity. **Gebrauchswert hoch im Kurs.**

Typography lives! It is not regarded today with the primacy of
Die Typografie lebt! Sie nimmt sich heute vielleicht nicht mehr so
perhaps 10 or 20 years ago, and is comprehended less as a "picture", but

0003
0096
wichtig wie vor 10 oder 20 Jahren, versteht sich weniger als Bild, tritt
rather, more as a "text". Nevertheless, it remains a prominent element of "visual
hinter den Text zurück. Trotzdem ist sie noch immer ein wichtiger Teil ‹visueller
communication": indispensable, and occasionally fresh, even original.
Kommunikation›: überall gefördert, ansehnlich und mitunter sogar noch
Currently: typography is still typography, although less
überraschend originell.

0097
0004
complacent, conceited, and self-confident, than in the late fifties. And,
Kurzum: die Typografie heute ist noch immer Typografie. Weniger
correspondingly, more functional, in that it has become completely adjusted
selbstgefällig, selbstbewusst und selbstsicher zwar als noch Ende der
to the rapid methods of mass communication.
fünfziger Jahre. Dafür aber ‹funktionaler›: in den schnellen Verwertungsprozess

0098
0005
This connotes "adapted": adapted to the developments
der Massenkommunikation voll eingepasst.
within the composing and print technologies; to the stipulations of an unstable
Das heisst: angepasst. Angepasst an die Erfordernisse neuerer Satz-
market; to the supposedly effective usage by the design profession; and
und Drucktechniken. An die Bedingungen schnell sich verändernder

0099
::
also adapted to a particularly unpleasant phenomenon of our profession: to design

Fortsetzung des Textes: Seite 4/Innenteil
Continuation of text: inside/page 14

TM (Typographische Monatsblätter)
Country: Switzerland
Cover Design: Wolfgang Weingart
Courtesy of syndicom

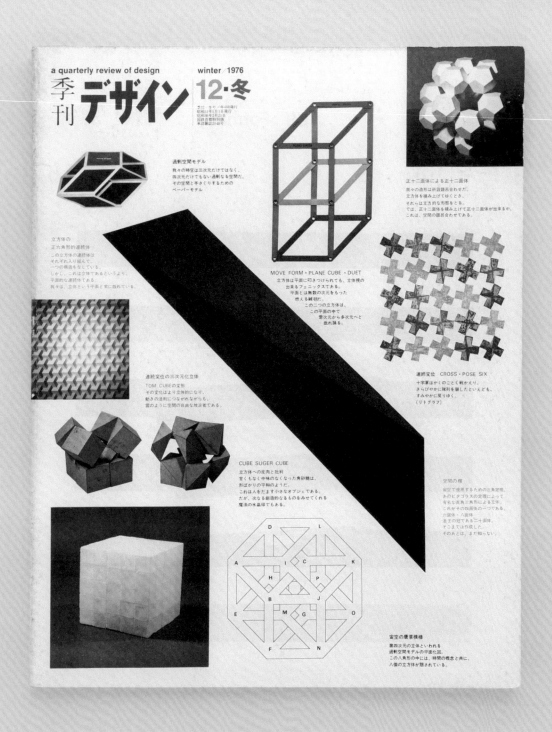

季刊デザイン

a quarterly review of design — winter / 1976

12・冬

過剰空間モデル

正十二面体による正十二面体

立方体の
正六角形の連続体

MOVE FORM・PLANE CUBE・DUET

連続変位の三次元化立体
TOM.CUBEの変形

連続変位 CROSS・POSE SIX

CUBE SUGER CUBE

空間の権

Design: A Quarterly
Review of Design
Country: Japan

Cover Painting: Hiroshi Tomura
Layout: Yuichi Tabuchi
Logo Type Design: Teijiro Nakade

035

Zeitschrift für verbale und visuelle Kommunikation   13. Jg. Heft 4   Juli 77   P 20638 F

68 ›**Format**›

Design_____Qualität vor Quantität und Originalität

Format
Country: Germany

Cover Design: Manfred Glemser

Typographic 10

Typographic is the journal of the Society of Typographic Designers

a e s r
Standard

a e s r
Airport

e e e

Standard Medium   Airport   Standard Bold

Airport, designed for the signage of London Heathrow in 1958 by Matthew Carter, is compared with Standard from which it is derived.

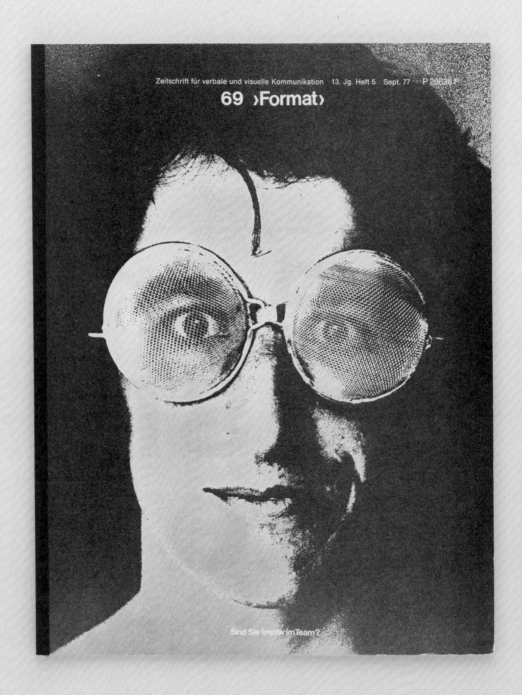

Zeitschrift für verbale und visuelle Kommunikation   13. Jg. Heft 5   Sept. 77   P 26636 F

69 ›Format›

Sind Sie kreativ im Team?

Format
Country: Germany

Cover Design: Grafik-Design Manz

A bi-annual Review of International Visual Communication Design

Issue number 11, 1977

ico**graphic** 11

Price of this issue 2.00 US dollars

Published in London by the International Council of Graphic Design Associations

Contents include

Divergent and convergent tendencies of the Latin and Cyrillic (Russian) alphabet

Probing pictures for a lingua franca
Posters for Peace by Israeli graphic design students
First steps on a thousand mile journey—part 2

The inadequacies of the Roman alphabet and a proposed phonetic alphabet with concept-related phonograms
Comenius and visual education

Patrick Wallis Burke

Z	W	E	E	F	V	L	I	E	G	T	U	I	G	R
(П)	(Д)	(Ф)	(Э)	(Й)	(Ж)	(Я)	E	K	R	A	B	E	P	
L	Y	N	V	L	I	E	G	T	U	I	G	P	A	A
(Ђ)	E	R	D	G	L	I	A	T	R	P	E	K	R	G
H	(Ж)	G	O	S	U	E	L	E	F	L	K	R	K	A
F	A	(Б)	E	T	T	O	E	L	S	E	Y	U	E	(Ћ)
K	R	R	(Ђ)	R	I	R	I	Y	T	T	R	I	(Й)	I
L	R	E	I	(Л)	W	N	O	B	F	T	R	(Я)	T	B
A	O	L	G	N	(Ч)	A	O	O	N	E	(Ж)	B	R	O
V	R	I	E	A	G	O	G	M	I	(Ф)	L	O	I	O
I	E	E	G	S	T	J	G	E	(Э)	W	U	O	R	T
S	T	R	R	S	A	O	A	(Ц)	N	E	A	T	E	W
A	T	T	A	R	L	U	(Ђ)	G	T	H	O	G	M	K
A	O	P	B	E	A	(Д)	T	T	E	L	J	E	E	P
K	K	A	V	A	(Ж)	J	E	O	V	R	K	A	A	N

Push Pin Graphic
Country: USA

Cover Design:
Seymour Chwast

Typographic

Journal of the Society of Typographic Designers

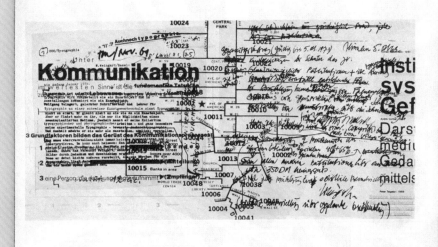

The typography of Wolfgang Weingart ▶

Collage: Wolfgang Weingart

U&lc
Country: USA

Cover Design:
Herb Lubalin Associates

Graphis
Country: Switzerland

Cover Design: Walter Ballmer

TM (Typographische Monatsblätter)
Country: Switzerland

Cover Design:
Jim Faris, Wolfgang Weingart
Courtesy of syndicom

U&lc.

INTERNATIONAL

Aa Bb Cc Dd Ee Ff Gg Hh Ii Jj Kk Ll Mm Nn Oo Pp   Qq Rr Ss Tt Uu Vv Ww Xx Yy Zz 1234567890&ÆŒ$¢£%!?()[]

UPPER AND LOWER CASE THE INTERNATIONAL JOURNAL OF TYPOGRAPHICS   PUBLISHED BY INTERNATIONAL TYPEFACE CORPORATION. VOLUME THREE, NUMBER TWO, JUNE, 1979

Art is just fine

PETER BEARD'S DIARY

BY CAROL DIGRAPPA

I first saw the remains of Peter Beard's diaries in November 1977 at the International Center of Photography. Earlier that year, over twenty years of diaries had been destroyed in a fire that razed Beard's Montauk windmill residence. Only two books survived. The 1976 **Bicentennial Diary**, which was at Meriden Gravure on the night of the fire, hung on the walls in lithographs—a colorful and portentous frieze in a bright white room. **The Elephant Diary**, filled with photographs dating from 1971 to 1976, had been with Beard the night of the fire and now lay open in a black box in the center of the room. The casket also held the soggy pile of burned books—ashes, mold and all.

Marvin Israel designed the show of diaries and dying elephants (from Beard's book **The End of the Game**) as a conceptual installation. To give the viewer the feeling of African imbalance, photographs of starved elephants, disintegrating carcasses, and ravaged land were theatrically lighted in the dark. Elephant dung, animal skulls, stress boxes jammed with progress reports from Kenya Colony, and jungle sounds carried out the themes of overpopulation, stress and destruction of habitat.

The elephants stood out as a metaphor for men. In contrast to the rest of the museum, the diary room seemed modern and light—an embellishment of the theme. The pages overlapped on the wall in a detailed bas-relief which, like death itself, seduced and repelled simultaneously.

After seeing pictures of so many rotting carcasses, the diaries conjured up a dream of the primeval forest—of a dense chaos. On each page, a wild landscape of "piddling trivia and absurdities" grew like a fungus. Each image was woven into another, blending and layering arcane truths and media nonsense until open space seemed as rare as in the forest, as meaningful as silence. Almost as if the diaries had designed themselves, they reflected a strange order in a complex growth of visions.

CONTINUED ON PAGE 3

045

U&lc
Country: USA

Cover Design:
Herb Lubalin Associates

グラフィック デザイン＋　September 1979 Autumn　75

Graphic Design
Country: Japan

Cover Design: Sato Koichi

Idea
Country: Japan

Cover Design: Wolfgang Weingart

Typos
Country: UK

Design Editors:
Usha Agarwal, Fred Lambert

Typos
Country: UK

Design Editors:
Usha Agarwal, Fred Lambert

Projekt
Country: Poland

Cover Art: Pawel Udorowiecki

Typografische Monatsblätter
Schweizer Grafische Mitteilungen
Revue suisse de l'imprimerie

Nr. 4/1980

400 Jahre Haas'sche Schriftgiesserei
400 ans de Fonderie de Caractères Haas
The Haas Typefoundry looks back on 400 years

TM (Typographische Monatsblätter)
Country: Switzerland
Design: unidentified
Courtesy of syndicom

THE ARCHITECTURAL REVIEW VOLUME CLXVII NUMBER 1000 JUNE 1980 UK £2·25

AR (The Architectural Review)
Country: UK

Cover Design: Philip Thompson

But above all astonishing inventions, what loftiness of mind was that of the man who conceived of finding a way to communicate his most recondite thoughts to whatever other person, although separated from him by the longest intervals of space and time! To speak with those who are in the Indies, to speak with those as yet unborn, or to be born perhaps a thousand or even ten thousand years hence! And with what ease! All through the various groupings of twenty simple characters on paper. *GALILEO*

New alphabets can only be a logical evolution of letterforms already existing, designed for modern techniques of composition and as an expression of our own time. Tomorrow's computerized photocomposition developments will demand new design systems prepared to the last detail, and we shall devise working solutions only if we dissociate ourselves from the outdated forms of the past. The world today changes more swiftly than it did in former decades. In this world the printed word will be an influence of tremendous power. And since the printing industry, like the other mass media — radio and television — can influence millions of people daily, it must remain fully aware of its responsibility. *HERMANN ZAPF*

U&lc
Country: USA

Cover Design:
Lubalin Peckolick Associates

Zeitschrift für verbale und visuelle Kommunikation   16. Jg. Heft 4   Juli 80   P 20638 F

86 ›Format›

Format
Country: Germany

Cover Design:
Prof. Herbert W Kapitzki

The Push Pin Graphic
Country: USA

Cover Design: John O'Leary

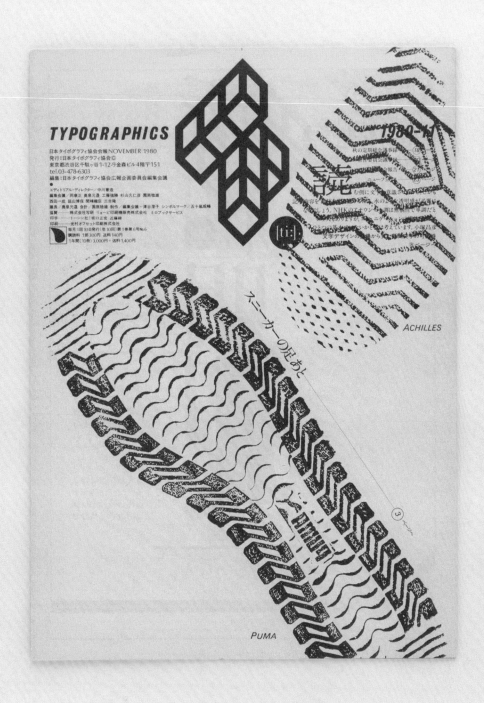

TYPOGRAPHICS

日本タイポグラフィ協会会報 NOVEMBER 1980
発行:日本タイポグラフィ協会 ©
東京都渋谷区千駄ヶ谷1-12-9金森ビル4階〒151
tel.03-478-6303
編集:日本タイポグラフィ協会広報企画委員会編集会議

エディトリアル・ディレクター/中川憲造
編集会議/岡庭正 奥泉元藤 工藤強勝 杉山久仁彦 園原敏雄
西川一成 益山博保 関峰嗣彦 三谷隆
協力/奥泉充造 会計/阪田雄雄 制作/編集会議・津谷澄子 シンボルマーク/五十嵐成棟
協賛/株式会社写研 リョービ印刷機販売株式会社 ミロブックサービス
印字/トーシン社/坂口正史 近藤峰
印刷/光村オフセット印刷株式会社

毎月(1回)30日発行(年10回)第1巻第6号No.6
購読料 1部300円 送料140円
1年間(10冊)3,000円・送料1,400円

1980-11

ACHILLES

PUMA

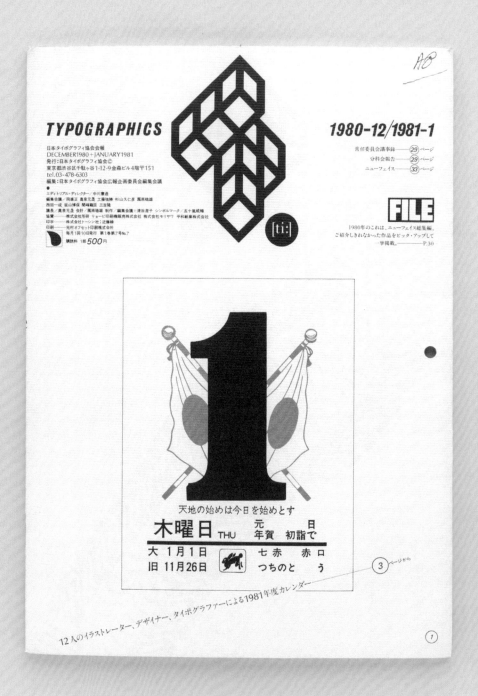

Typographics Ti
Country: Japan

Design: unidentified

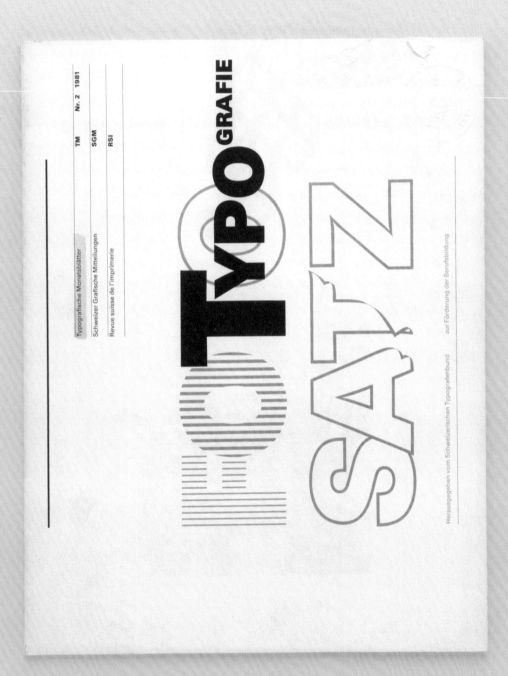

TM (Typographische Monatsblätter)
Country: Switzerland

Cover Design:
Heinrich Fleischhacker
Courtesy of syndicom

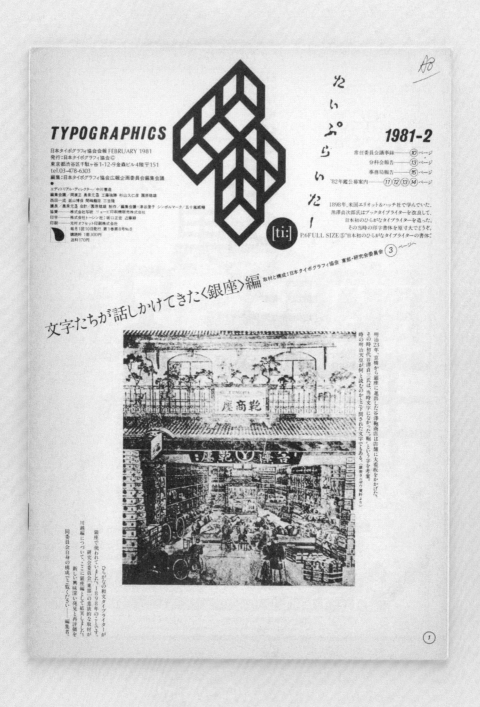

Typographics Ti
Country: Japan

Design: unidentified

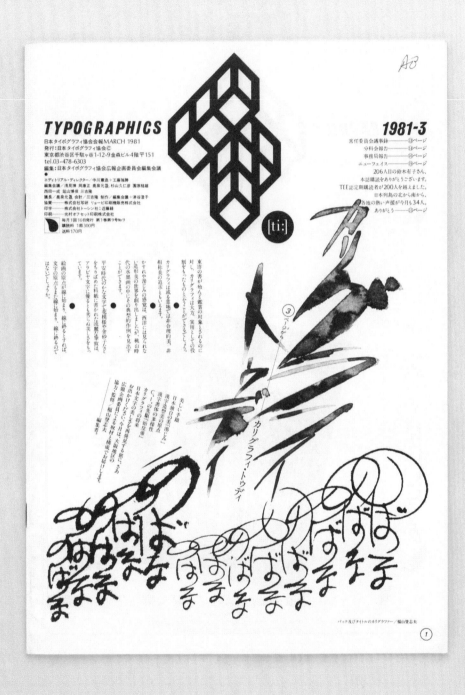

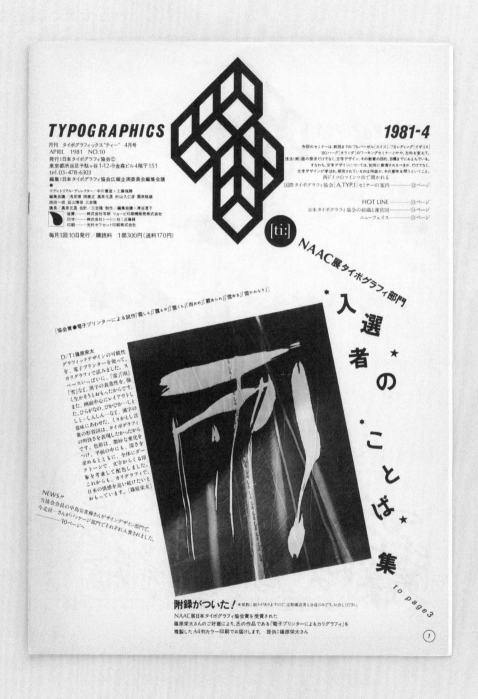

Typographics Ti
Country: Japan

Design: unidentified

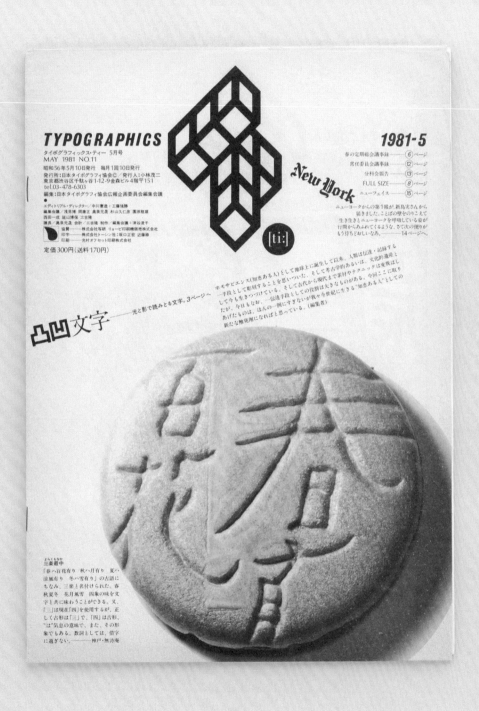

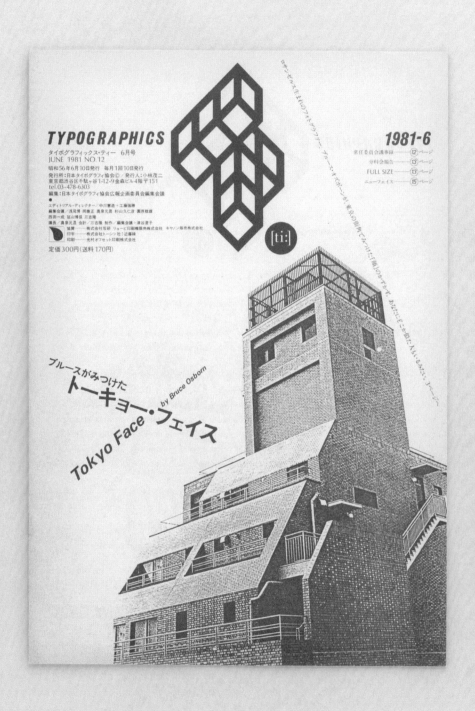

Typographics Ti
Country: Japan

Design: unidentified

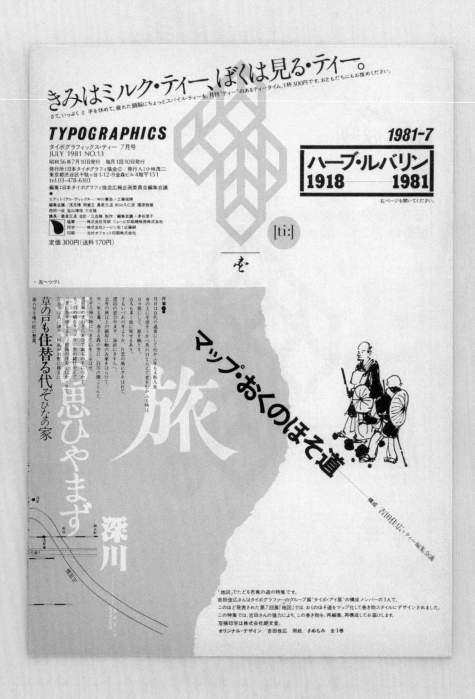

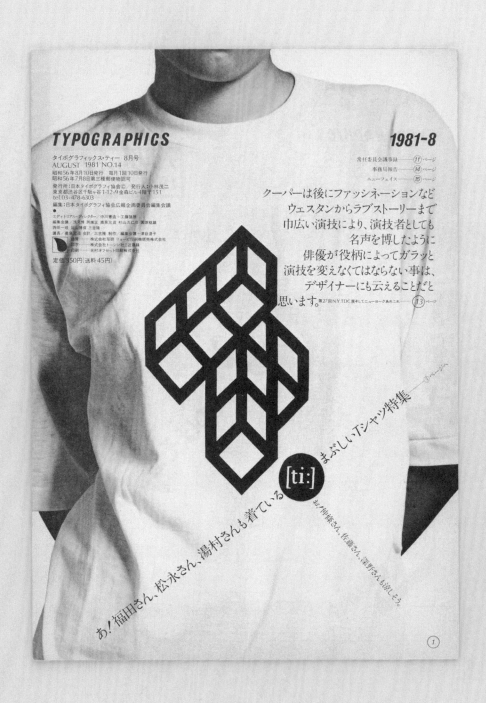

Typographics Ti
Country: Japan

Design: unidentified

09—11.1981

TYPOS

Typos
Country: UK

Design Editors:
Usha Agarwal, Fred Lambert

067

10.1981

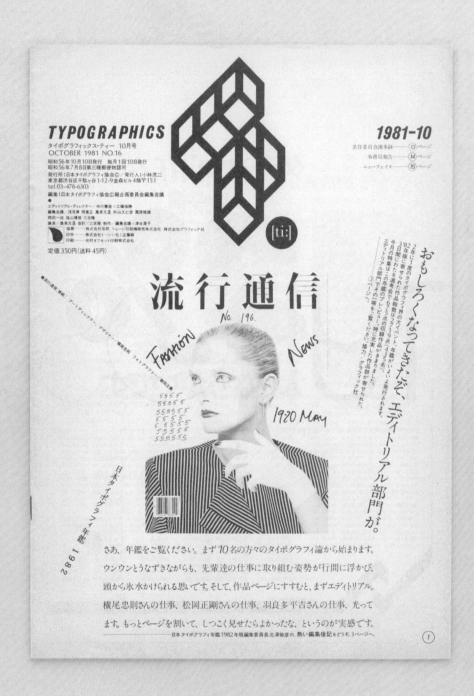

Typographics Ti
Country: Japan

Design: unidentified

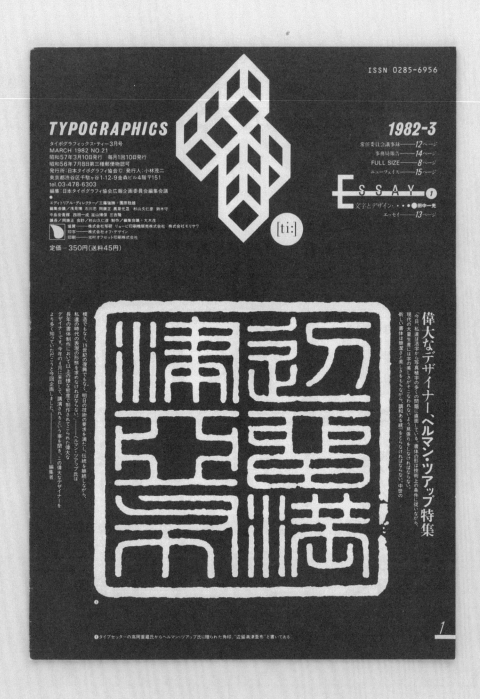

ISSN 0285-6956

TYPOGRAPHICS

タイポグラフィックス・ティー・3月号
MARCH 1982 NO 21
昭和57年3月10日発行 毎月1回10日発行
昭和56年7月8日第三種郵便物認可
発行所:日本タイポグラフィ協会Ⓒ 発行人:小林茂二
東京都渋谷区千駄ヶ谷1-12-9金森ビル4階 〒151
tel.03-478-6303
編集:日本タイポグラフィ協会広報企画委員会編集会議

エディトリアル・ディレクター／工藤強勝・園原牧雄
編集会議／浅葉隆 石川忠 岡嶋正 奥野光哉 杉山久仁彦 鈴木守
中島英樹 西田一成 蚤山博保 三吉隆
講賞／岡倉正 会計／杉山久仁彦 制作／編集会議・大木茂
協賛―――――株式会社写研 リョービ印刷機販売株式会社 株式会社モリサワ
印字―――――株式会社オフ・デザイン
印刷―――――光村オフセット印刷株式会社

定価――350円(送料45円)

[ti:]

1982-3

常任委員会議事録――――12ページ
事務局報告―――――14ページ
FULL SIZE――――――8ページ
ニューフェイス――――15ページ

ESSAY ①
文字とデザイン・・・●田中一光
エッセイ――13ページ

偉大なデザイナー、ヘルマン・ツァップ特集

今日 私達は活字から写真植字の多くの問題に直面している。書体の形は技術の条件に従いながら、現代の大量生産は本の美しさも失われないという状況を作り上げたが、新しい書体は描法される美しさをもちながら、調和ある続一をとらなければならない。中世の

横道でもなく、19世紀の復興でもなく、明日の技術の要求を満たし、伝統を継承しながら、私達はこの時代の表現の形態を求めなければならない。――ヘルマン・ツァップ

長年の書体制作において以上の様な態度で制作されてきたこの偉大なデザイナーです。今年の4月に来日して、講演されるという事を聞き、この偉大なデザイナーをより多く知っていただこうと今回企画しました。――編集者

●タイプセッターの高岡重蔵氏からヘルマン・ツァップ氏に贈られた角印、"辺留満津亜布"と書いてある

1

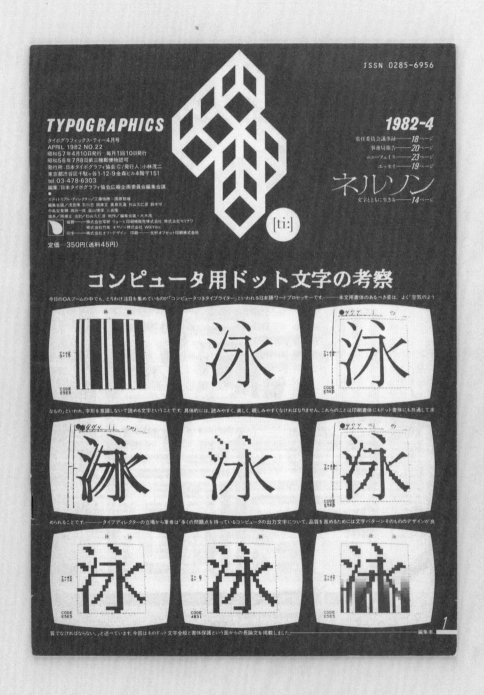

Typographics Ti
Country: Japan
Design: unidentified

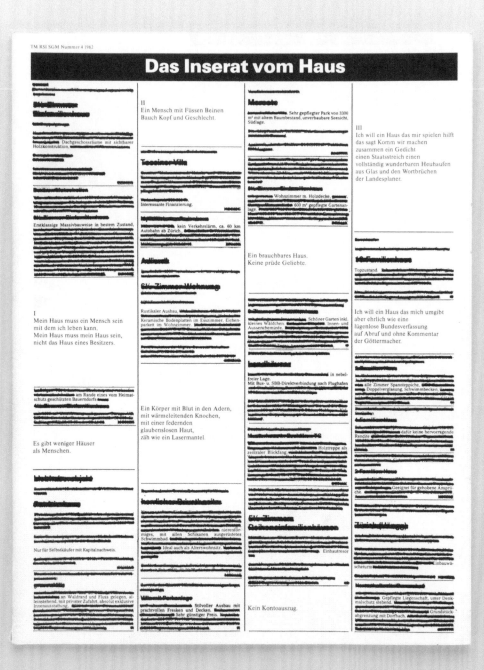

TM (Typographische Monatsblätter)
Country: Switzerland

Cover Design: Dora Wespi
Courtesy of syndicom

Lecturis Documentaire
Country: Netherlands

Cover Design: Bart de Groot

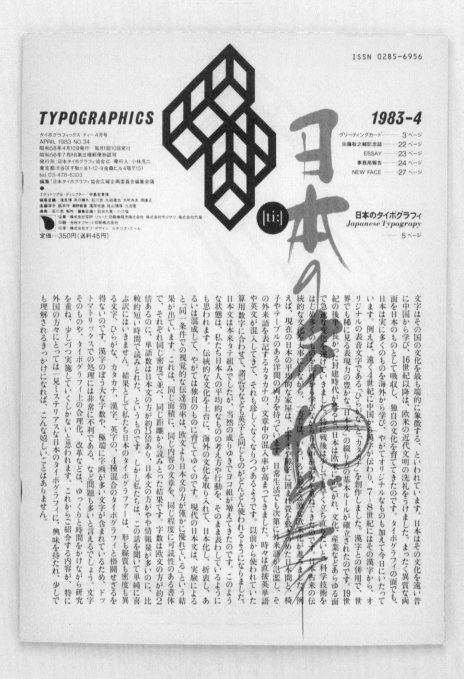

Typographics Ti
Country: Japan

Design: unidentified

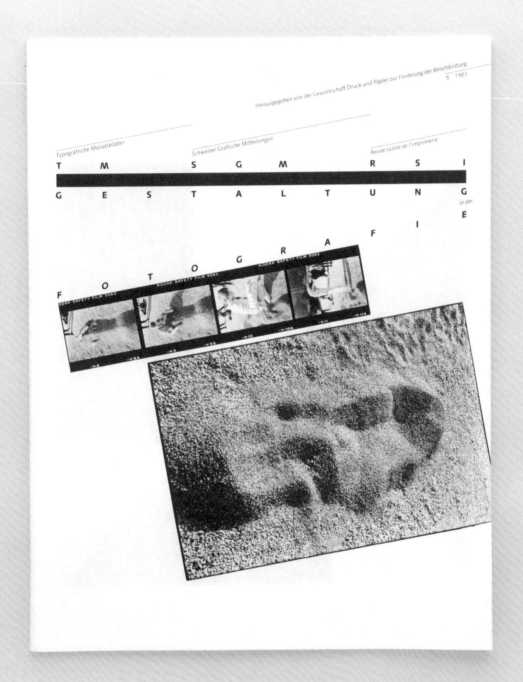

Idea
Country: Japan

Cover Design: Walter Allner

Typographic

The Journal of the Society of Typographic Designers
Issue Number 23 December 1983   £1.95

Typographics Ti
Country: Japan

Design: unidentified

Q *Emigre* (1984–2005, USA) played a crucial role in establishing the notion that a designer could be more than just the layout person for a publication. *Emigre* proved that designers could also be editors and publishers. Was this your intention when you started *Emigre*?

A Not consciously. But as a designer I quickly realised that you hold many keys to publishing a magazine. Design is a crucial component of the publishing process. Then, as I worked at all kinds of design odd jobs, for various publishers and other entrepreneurs, and looked behind the scenes, I often found that what my clients did to put out their product wasn't exactly rocket science. It just took a lot of guts, hard work, money and perseverance. At some point I must have thought: I could do that myself. Instead of being a cog in the machine, I could be the machine.

I always felt attracted to designers who took on the challenges and responsibilities of putting out their own products. I was very intrigued by the entire process of publishing, not just the design of a cover, or a layout, but also the manufacturing, distribution, financing, advertising; all the aspects of publishing necessary to put ideas out in the world. And we were doing this in an era that was rich with a DIY attitude. It was the halcyon days of small independent record labels, distributors and publishers. Designers are very resourceful, they are good at problem-solving, they're natural editors, and they're curious. It's a perfect fit for putting out your own products.

Q *Emigre* is often cited as the first design publication of the computerised era in design. What role did computerisation play in the magazine's evolution?

A The most immediate impact of computerisation for us was on the cost of typesetting. Up to the point of the arrival of the Mac we either used professional photo typesetting services, which was far beyond our non-existent budget, or we used typewriters, Letraset, and cut-and-paste to set our texts. With the Mac we could make our own fonts. Granted, they were coarse resolution bitmap fonts, and many designers thought they looked hideous. But to us it was a way to save money on typesetting, and as an added bonus we were able to differentiate ourselves from every other magazine simply because of those curious never-before-seen typefaces that we used.

The first time we used the Mac for *Emigre*, in 1985, there were no page layout programmes; Postscript and Laser printers didn't even exist yet. We printed out low-resolution type on an image writer on paper as big as we could, and then we reduced the type using a stat camera and pasted it down on boards. It was a slow and gradual transition from manual paste-up to full computerisation. It wasn't until ten years later, probably around 1996, that we did our first issue where layouts and pre-press, including images, were done entirely digitally.

As the computer became more sophisticated, so did our typefaces, and before long requests were coming in from designers asking if they could purchase the fonts that we were using in *Emigre* magazine. That's how the Emigre fonts foundry came about. We initially sold typesetting to designers using our fonts. Then later we started selling the fonts on floppy disks. The sales of those typefaces is what largely supported the publishing of *Emigre* magazine. And then, when the Internet came along, we couldn't believe our luck. We had a successful digital product that we could now sell online. So now the computer was the machine that we used to design, manufacture, and distribute our product. So in terms of the evolution of *Emigre*, the computer had an impact on how we designed, but much more significantly it was central to how we operated as a business.

Q What publications did you regard as role models when you started out in 1984?

A When we started *Emigre* there was a plethora of independently published magazines. A trip to Printed Matter in New York in those days was always like a treasure hunt for independently published magazines. There are too many to mention. I remember closely studying *4 Taxis* (1978–86, France), I loved *RAW* (1980–91, USA), and I still have copies of *Wet* (1976–81, USA) magazine. But it was *Hard Werken* (1978–82, Netherlands) that inspired

Hard Werken
1978–82
Netherlands

me the most. I tried to mimic that as best I could without looking like a complete copycat.

Q How do you view the current publication landscape regarding graphic design writing and critical engagement?

A I'm always searching, but I find it's slim pickings. I'm impressed with *Slanted* (2004–present, Germany) and *Azimuth* (France); *Idea* (1953–present, Japan) continues to impress me, although the latter is almost entirely a visual treat for me. Lately, I have found the most interesting writing on design in exhibition catalogues, like Andrew Blauvelt and Ellen Lupton's *Graphic Design: Now in Production* or Jon Sueda's exhibition catalogues such as *All Possible Futures*. There may be other great writing out there, but I don't know where it's hiding. In general I'm at a loss to know what the prevailing conversations within design are about these days. There used to be a time when someone like Steven Heller could write an article about 'ugly' design and there'd be a firestorm that lasted for years. It's been a while since I've seen anything like that.

Q A favourite *Emigre* cover and a favourite non-*Emigre* design magazine cover?

A That's always difficult, but I do still like the cover of *Emigre* No.1 (shown over). Runner-up would be No.24 (p.133). My favourite non-*Emigre* cover, for a design magazine, probably Wolfgang Weingart's covers for *Typographische Monatsblätter* (1932–90, Switzerland).

Rudy VanderLans is a Dutch graphic designer who co-founded Emigre with his wife Zuzana Licko in 1984. Emigre was a journal for experimental graphic design, and pioneered the development of fonts on the Mac.

Idea
1953—present
Japan

TM
1932—present
Switzerland

EMIGRE

(A Magazine for Exiles)

Emigre
Country: USA

Design: Rudy VanderLans
Fonts: Zuzana Licko

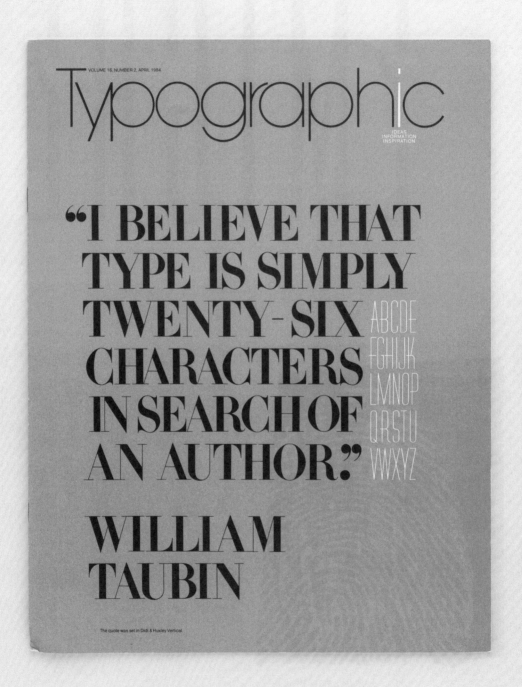

VOLUME 16, NUMBER 2, APRIL 1984

Typographic

IDEAS
INFORMATION
INSPIRATION

"I BELIEVE THAT TYPE IS SIMPLY TWENTY-SIX CHARACTERS IN SEARCH OF AN AUTHOR."

ABCDE
FGHIJK
LMNOP
QRSTU
VWXYZ

WILLIAM TAUBIN

The quote was set in Didi & Huxley Vertical

Typographic-i
Country: USA

Cover Design: Pat Taylor

TM (Typographische Monatsblätter)
Country: Switzerland

Cover Design: Jean-Pierre Graber.
Courtesy of syndicom

Weingart:

My Typography Instruction at the Basle School of Design/Switzerland 1968 to 1985.

**Design
Quarterly**

130

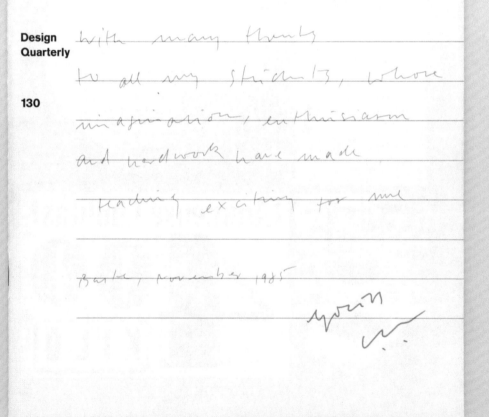

Design Quarterly
Country: USA

Cover Design: Armin Hofmann,
Wolfgang Weingart
Courtesy the Walker Art Centre.

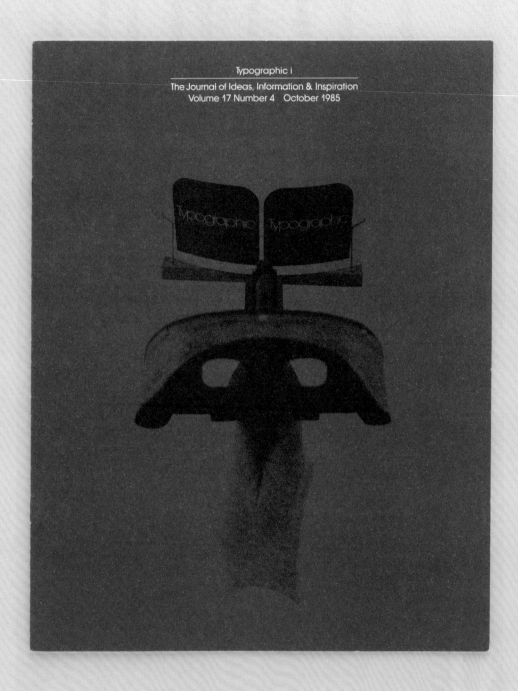

Typographic i

The Journal of Ideas, Information & Inspiration
Volume 17 Number 4   October 1985

EMIGRE

THE MAGAZINE THAT IGNORES BOUNDARIES

Michelle Vignes, Alice Poleski, Yul Brynner, John Hersey, Grant Muruaga, Anne Gleeson, Marc Susan, Lisa Cohen, Samuel Beckett, Dana F. Smith, John Fante, Antonio Ole, Andrei Toluzakov, Lewis MacAdams, Svetlana Darsalia, Didier Cremieux, Marek Majevski, Gavin Flint, Tom Clark, Peter Plate, James Joyce, William Cone, Christopher Marlowe, Menno Meyjes, Badri E. Borghei, Bijan Samandar, F. Heidari.

3

Emigre
Country: USA

Design: Rudy VanderLans
Fonts: Zuzana Licko

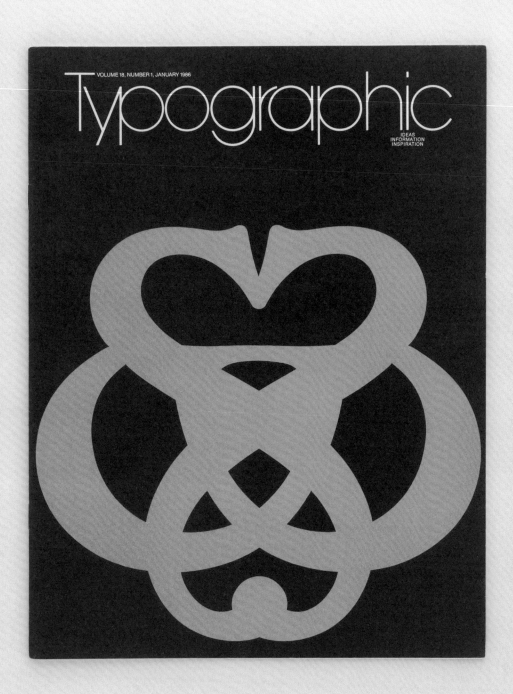

VOLUME 18, NUMBER 1, JANUARY 1986

Typographic

IDEAS
INFORMATION
INSPIRATION

Typographic-i
Country: USA

Design: unidentified

Octavo
Country: UK

Cover Design: 8vo

Q Does the graphic designer of a design magazine – I'm thinking mainly of the covers here – have a freedom not enjoyed by the designers of magazine covers for a non-design audience?

A In communication terms, no. In execution terms, yes. Magazine covers, whatever the audience, need to convey a message or story, or simply a list of contents. The design needs to be attention grabbing, yet decipherable. Of course there are always exceptions that succeed in breaking the rules. Designing a cover for a design audience can allow you to take a few liberties or be a little experimental, building on the mutual level of visual understanding between audience and reader.

Q Is there a sense in which designing for designers is easy? Or, to put it another way, does it lead to self-indulgence when we know our audience is made up of designers?

A Often, designing for other designers is tough. They're an exacting bunch and highly critical. With a design audience there's sometimes the feeling of wanting to do something that little bit special, the unseen. With that comes the need for constraint, otherwise self-indulgence can surface. I like to think good designers at some point swore their allegiance to the communication oath and if self-indulgence occurs then they quickly learn from it and move on. Having said that, self-indulgence is not always bad. Designers are a savvy bunch – they know the pitfalls. You could say there's a fine line between self-indulgence and the experimentation necessary to carrying the creative professions forward.

Q What and who were your influences when you started *Octavo* (1986–92, UK)?

A From my own perspective it was Simon Johnston and Hamish Muir, my two 8vo partners and co-editors, and Michael Burke. They each had a deeper understanding of the European design tradition. Simon and Hamish had spent time studying under Weingart, and Mike had worked with Otl Aicher and Rolf Müller on the Munich Olympics. I had spent three years in San Francisco around new-wave Postmodernism but there was something about it I disliked enormously. Perhaps it was its slickness. In the early days of 8vo I was influenced by the directness, rule breaking and authenticity of European Modernism which I was introduced to by Simon and Hamish. It was the real thing. Prior to 8vo my knowledge of other designers here and abroad was nominal, and my exposure to Europe limited. In design school, I knew of Total Design and Studio Dumbar, and the work of leading illustrators like Bush Hollyhead, George Hardie, Sue Coe and Ian Pollock, all of whom I was fortunate enough to study under, and all of whom I respected enormously while I railed against the paucity of the vocational design teaching in north-east England. I was acutely aware of the commercialised nature of the late-1970s London design scene, and it was that which made me move abroad. I was too full of angst at college to be influenced, and during my time in San Francisco too busy paying the rent and too busy trying to find work, which was never easy, being an 'illegal alien'. When I came back to London I was 26, battle hardened and more ready than ever to take on the world. The chance to form a company like 8vo couldn't come fast enough. I had limitless drive, enthusiasm, passion and ambition. I knew it was my time and I knew I had to grab the opportunity.

Q Could *Octavo* exist today in the age of the Internet – and is there anyone carrying on the work you started?

A I think there's a developed understanding now with regard to electronic and printed books, and how the two survive and operate alongside each other. There are parallels in music – MP3 for convenience and vinyl for experience. Print will always offer a different kind of experience to digital and it's that realisation that has led to many non-fiction and design printed books becoming objectified in their design. Of course *Octavo* could exist in some form on the Internet today but I don't think it would be the ideal place for it, and it probably wouldn't be the same publication. It was a design-led journal and was very

Octavo
1986–92
UK

Octavo
1986–92
UK

much designed to be held in the hand. It had an 'object' quality and one of its principal aims was to raise the bar in terms of typographic execution, repro, printing and finishing.

Regarding today's practitioners, I'm sure there are many working with the intention to produce equally experiential print. In some ways the practice is more widespread now because of the impact of the Internet. I wouldn't say there is anyone specifically carrying on the work we started with *Octavo* – they would have to be nuts to do so, especially if they were doing that kind of work in a self-published way, outside of their studio work. They would need unshakeable, long-term conviction. The advantage of the Internet, though, is that they wouldn't necessarily need deep-lined pockets.

Q Can you name some outstanding design magazine covers?
A During a recent visit to the Stedelijk Museum I enjoyed the covers of *S+RO* (*Stedenbouw & Ruimtelijke Ordening*), published by the Netherlands Institute of Urbanism and Spatial Planning in The Hague. Helmut Schmid's covers for *Grafisk Revy* (1930–36, Scandinavia) are a highlight for me, as are the two years of covers for *TM* (*Typografische Monatsblätter*) (1932–present, Switzerland), produced by Weingart in 1972 and 1973. I too liked the early, large format covers of Warhol's *Interview* (1969–present, US) magazine, the paper surface being such a contradiction to the image they were conveying.

Mark Holt is a graphic designer and co-founder of 8vo design studio and Octavo *magazine.*

TM
1932—present
Switzerland

TM
1932—present
Switzerland

090

86.2

octavo

journal of typography

second of eight issues

Octavo
Country: UK

Cover Design: 8vo

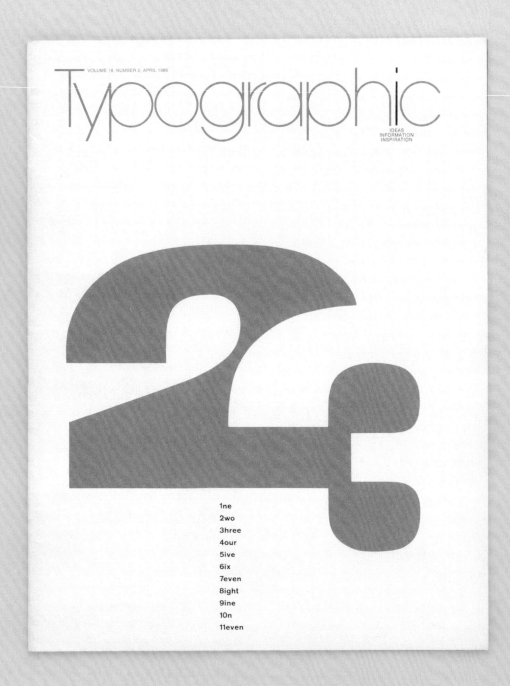

VOLUME 18, NUMBER 2, APRIL 1986

Typographic

IDEAS
INFORMATION
INSPIRATION

1ne
2wo
3hree
4our
5ive
6ix
7even
8ight
9ine
10n
11even

Typographic-i
Country: USA

Design: unidentified

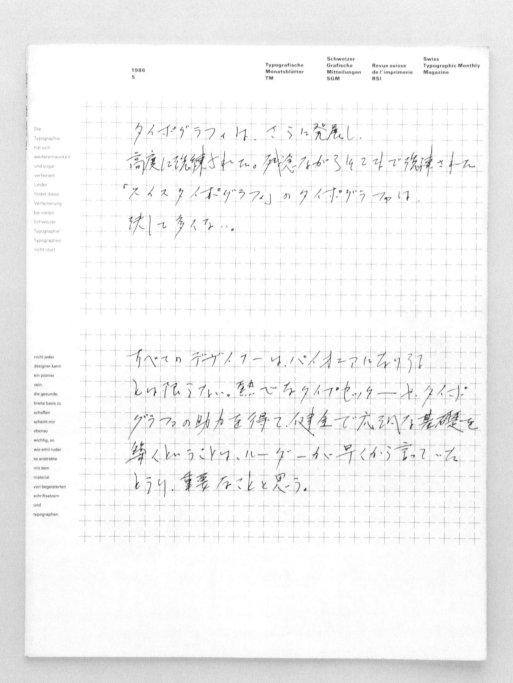

1986
5

Typografische
Monatsblätter
TM

Schweizer
Grafische
Mitteilungen
SGM

Revue suisse
de l'imprimerie
RSI

Swiss
Typographic Monthly
Magazine

Die
Typographie
hat sich
weiterentwickelt
und sogar
verfeinert
Leider
findet diese
Verfeinerung
bei vielen
'Schweizer
Typographie'
Typographen
nicht statt

nicht jeder
designer kann
ein pionier
sein.
die gesunde,
breite basis zu
schaffen
scheint mir
ebenso
wichtig, so
wie emil ruder
es anstrebte
mit dem
material
von begeisterten
schriftsetzern
und
typographen.

TM (Typographische Monatsblätter)   Cover Design: Helmut Schmid
Country: Switzerland   Courtesy of syndicom

Q Which were the early influential magazines of the 20th century?

A Before they got to build anything, the architectural avant-garde started magazines that served as manifestos – personal, as well as philosophical. They had a way of annexing as much cultural territory as possible, spreading into art and literature. In the Netherlands, Theo van Doesburg published *De Stijl* from 1917 to 1920, and in so doing triggered a movement that took in Piet Mondrian and Gerrit Rietveld, although, as is the way of such things, some were reluctant to see themselves labelled as part of a school.

Le Corbusier knew *De Stijl*, and when he got to Paris started *L'Esprit Nouveau* with the painter Amédée Ozenfant, that ran from 1920 to 1925. In its pages appeared much of the text that Le Corbusier later published as *Vers une architecture* (1923, France), perhaps the most influential architectural book of the 20th century. It was here that Le Corbusier suggested that a house should be regarded as a machine for living. Literature, poetry and art were all covered, including contributions from Fernand Léger. It was here that Le Corbusier collaged images of a Farman Goliath biplane with Notre Dame, and a photograph of the Arc de Triomphe with a Cunard liner.

In Germany, *G* (1923–26, Germany) was started by Hans Richter and El Lissitzky. No.3, from 1924, had Mies van der Rohe's glass skyscraper on its cover. The English, by and large, were unmoved. In Evelyn Waugh's *Decline and Fall* (1928), the sinister Otto Silenus comes to the attention of Margot Beste-Chetwynde in the pages of a progressive Hungarian quarterly, and demolishes her exquisite stately home to make way for 'a surprising creation of ferro-concrete and aluminium'.

Q Which journals became the dominant voices in mid-20th century European and USA architecture?

A In Italy, editing a magazine was seen as an essential part of architectural practice. *Domus* (1928–present, Italy) set the pattern, established by Gio Ponti and edited by him with occasional interruptions until his death in 1979. Ponti's skills ran from illustrating the cover to designing the Pirelli tower. Ernest Rogers wrote his leader outlining his belief that design was a continuum, from the city to the spoon. *Casabella* (1928–present, Italy) was started shortly after *Domus*, and provided a sharper modernist focus.

Anglo-American mid-century magazines were never as closely associated with the individual practice of an architect. In California, *Arts and Architecture* (1929–67, USA), under the editorship of John Entenza, was hugely influential in promoting Charles and Ray Eames. The magazine was behind the Case Study houses programme, a series of low-cost individual houses that demonstrated what modern architecture had to offer, and established a specifically Californian approach.

The Architectural Review (1896–present, UK) is the grand old lady of architectural publishing, established in the 19th century. Its pages have acted as a place of record more than as a polemic for the work of particular individuals, or serving as a calling card for architects/editors. In the 1950s and 1960s its graphic treatments influenced the Italians. *Architectural Design* (1930–present, USA) in the 1970s was transformed from a competitor to the *AR* for the middle ground, and became an insight into the world of inflatables, domes and radical technology, along the lines of the *Whole Earth Catalog* (1968–1972, and intermittently thereafter, USA).

Q Which publications inspired you in the early days of *Blueprint* (1983–present, USA) and what made it new and different?

A The idea for *Blueprint* came from Peter Murray. He wanted to call it *High Point*, but I thought *Blueprint* was a better idea. The newspaper format was a deliberate attempt to make it less of a showcase, and have the ability to be irreverent or polemical. Publish anything on coated paper with high production values and you are somehow endorsing it. *Blueprint* wanted to be able to attack as well as persuade. It took the idea from *Skyline* (1978–80, USA) (designed by Massimo Vignelli), one of two or three tabloid formats around at the start of the 1980s. It suspended publishing just before our first issue.

**Domus
1928–present
Italy**

**Casabella
1928–present
Italy**

We also put faces on the cover, which seemed like a new idea, with the intention that we could somehow humanise the subject. We seemed to develop a curse on the subjects. Almost every architectural partnership we photographed for the cover broke up. The range of subject matter in *Blueprint* certainly came from *Domus*: we published art and design as well as architecture. But *Domus* had a budget, and for the first year everybody – designers, writers and photographers and illustrators – worked for love.

Q *Domus had a very distinctive and celebrated approach to design of their covers under your editorship: could you talk a little about them?*

A Simon Esterson and I have worked together for a long time. He taught me a lot about how to edit a magazine. He had a great way of telling stories by placing pictures effectively with words. We never had lengthy conversations about layouts: he had perfect pitch in laying out spreads to take you through an individual building, or a reportage on Beijing, or a monograph on an individual such as Shiro Kuramata. The thing about *Domus* is that its publishers see their role as selecting an editor and then letting them get on with it. We wanted to create a look for the magazine that made it clear it was *Domus*, and one that was calmer than it had been before.

Deyan Sudjic is director of the Design Museum in London. He was a founding editor of Blueprint, *and editor at* Domus *for four years. His career spans journalism, teaching and writing, across architecture and design.*

AD
1930—present
UK

Blueprint
1983—present
UK

THE LEADING MAGAZINE OF ARCHITECTURE AND DESIGN / JUNE 1986 / NUMBER 28 / £1.50

BLUEPRINT

FOSTER TAKES OFF AT STANSTED
MY OTHER SUNGLASSES ARE A PORSCHE

STEPHEN BAYLEY TAKES IT OUT ON WILLIAM MORRIS

HOW DESIGN GREW TO BE BIG BUSINESS

SIR TERENCE CONRAN PHOTOGRAPHED BY PHIL SAYER

Typografische Monatsblätter
Schweizer Grafische Mitteilungen
Zeitschrift für Schriftsatz, Gestaltung,
Sprache, Druck und
Weiterverarbeitung
Herausgegeben von der Gewerkschaft
Druck und Papier
zur Förderung der Berufsbildung

Revue suisse de l'imprimerie
Revue pour la composition,
la conception graphique, la langue,
l'impression et l'apprêt
Editée par le Syndicat du livre
et du papier
pour l'éducation professionnelle

Swiss Typographic Monthly
Magazine
Journal for Typographic Composition,
Design, Communication, Printing
and Production
Published by the Printing and
Paper Union of Switzerland
for the advancement of education
in the profession

6 1986

TM SGM RSI

TM (Typographische Monatsblätter)   Cover Design: Max Caflisch
Country: Switzerland   Courtesy of syndicom

TYP (Typografisch Papier)
Country: Netherlands

Cover Design: Max Kisman

1E JAARGANG NUMMER A NOVEMBER 1986

TYPOGRAFISCH PAPIER

DE COMPUTER INSPIREERT

TYP (Typografisch Papier)
Country: Netherlands   Cover Design: Max Kisman

EUROPE'S LEADING MAGAZINE OF ARCHITECTURE AND DESIGN / DECEMBER-JANUARY 1986 / NUMBER 23 / £1.50

BLUEPRINT

CRISTIAN CIRICI: THE MAN WHO RE-BUILT MIES. PHOTOGRAPH BY DAVID BANKS

BORN AGAIN BARCELONA

PLUS MICHAEL GRAVES EXCLUSIVE AND DAN DARE VERSUS JUDGE DREDD

Typografische Monatsblätter
Schweizer Grafische Mitteilungen

Zeitschrift für Schriftsatz, Gestaltung,
Sprache, Druck
und Weiterverarbeitung

Herausgegeben von der Gewerkschaft
Druck und Papier
zur Förderung der Berufsbildung

Revue suisse de l'imprimerie

Revue pour la composition,
la conception graphique, la langue,
l'impression et l'apprêt

Editée par le Syndicat du livre
et du papier
pour l'éducation professionnelle

Swiss Typographic Monthly
Magazine

Journal for Typographic Composition,
Design, Communication, Printing
and Production

Published by the Printing and Paper Union
of Switzerland for the advancement
of education in the profession

1 1987

TM (Typographische Monatsblätter)
Country: Switzerland

Cover Design:
Jean-Pierre Graber
Courtesy of syndicom

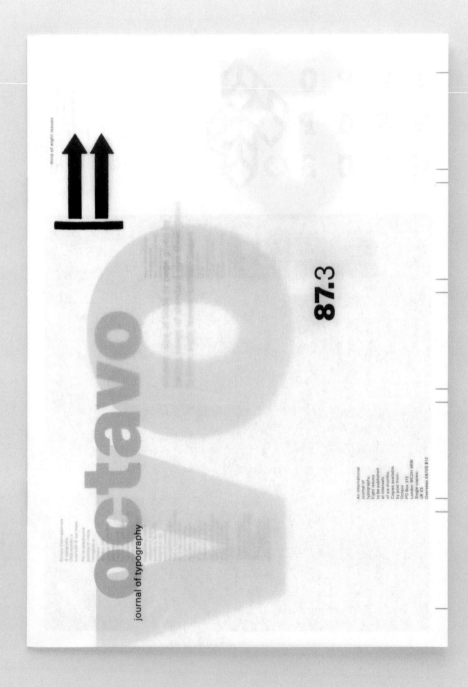

Typographics Ti
Country: Japan

Design: unidentified

Octavo 87.4 the fourth of eight issues, features Wolfgang Weingart's historic 1972 illustrated lecture manuscript 'How Can One Make Swiss Typography?' Previously only available in a limited photocopied edition, this seminal work has been updated and its importance reassessed fifteen years on, in a new introduction written by the author.

octavo

Octavo
Country: UK

Cover Design: 8vo

Emigre
Country: USA

Design: Rudy VanderLans
Fonts: Zuzana Licko

TYP (Typografisch Papier)
Country: Netherlands

Cover Design: Max Kisman

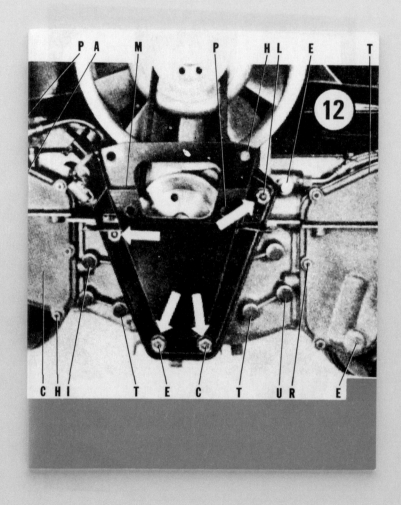

PAMPHLET ARCHITECTURE

Pamphlet Architecture
Country: USA

Cover Design: Neil Denari

Emigre
Country: USA

Design: Rudy VanderLans
Fonts: Zuzana Licko

TWEEDE JAARGANG / NUMMER C / NOVEMBER 1987

TYPOGRAFISCH PAPIER

TYP (Typografisch Papier)
Country: Netherlands

Cover Design: Max Kisman

TWEEDE JAARGANG / NUMMER C / NOVEMBER 1987

TYP (Typografisch Papier)
Country: Netherlands

Cover Design: Max Kisman

THE LEADING MAGAZINE OF ARCHITECTURE AND DESIGN/APRIL 1988/NUMBER 46/£2

BLUEPRINT

ESPRIT IN LONDON/THE CUCKOO CLOCK AS ARCHITECTURE

SPECIAL ISSUE
BRITISH GRAPHICS
THE VISUAL LANGUAGE
OF NEVILLE BRODY
THE GUARDIAN
FROM COMMERCIAL ART
TO PLAIN COMMERCIAL

PHOTOGRAPH OF NEVILLE BRODY BY NICK KNIGHT

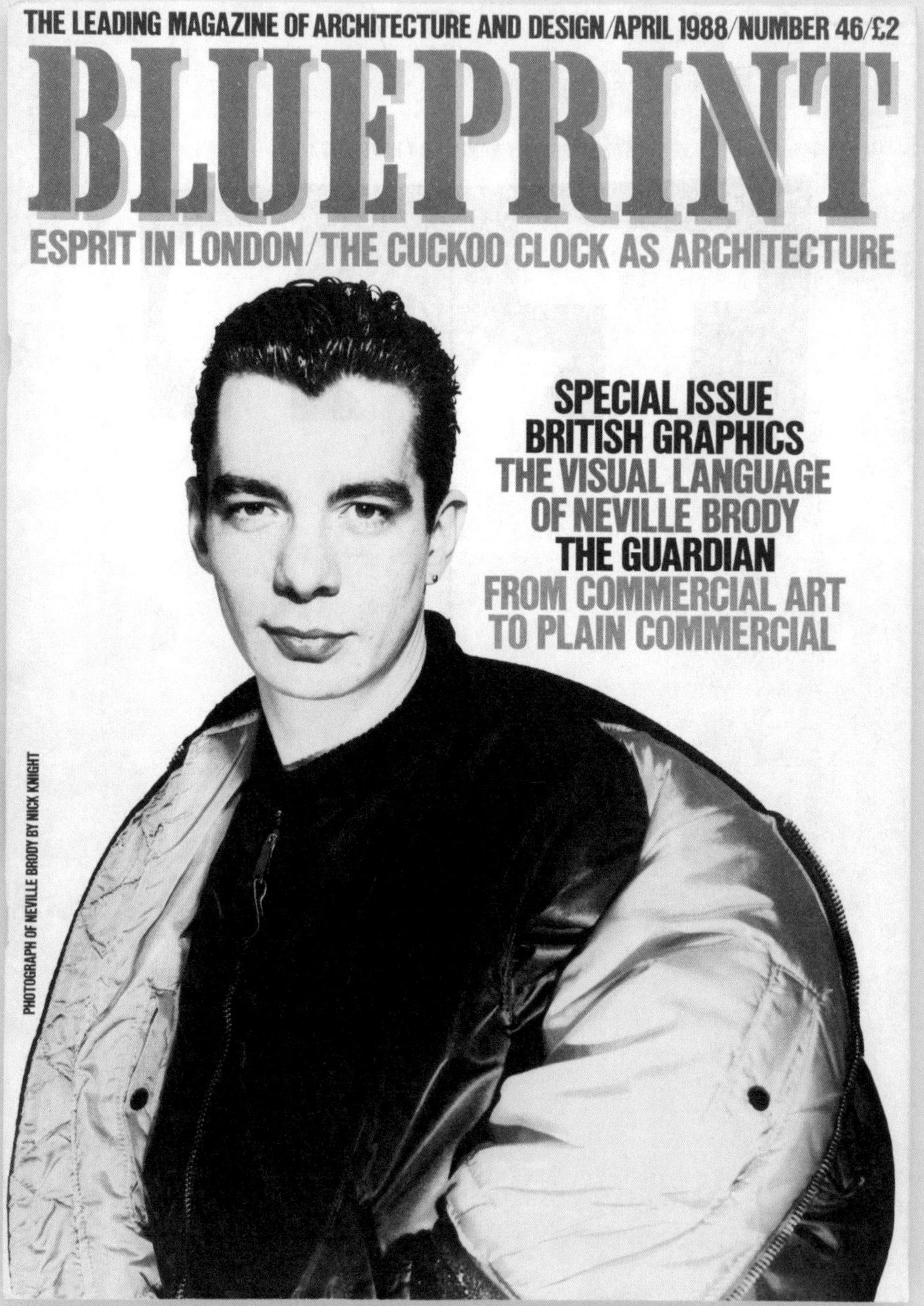

Blueprint
Country: UK

Art Editors:
Stephen Coates, Simon Esterson
Photography: Nick Knight

Emigre
Country: USA

Design: Rudy VanderLans
Fonts: Zuzana Licko

1988

Octavo
Country: UK

Cover Design: 8vo

115

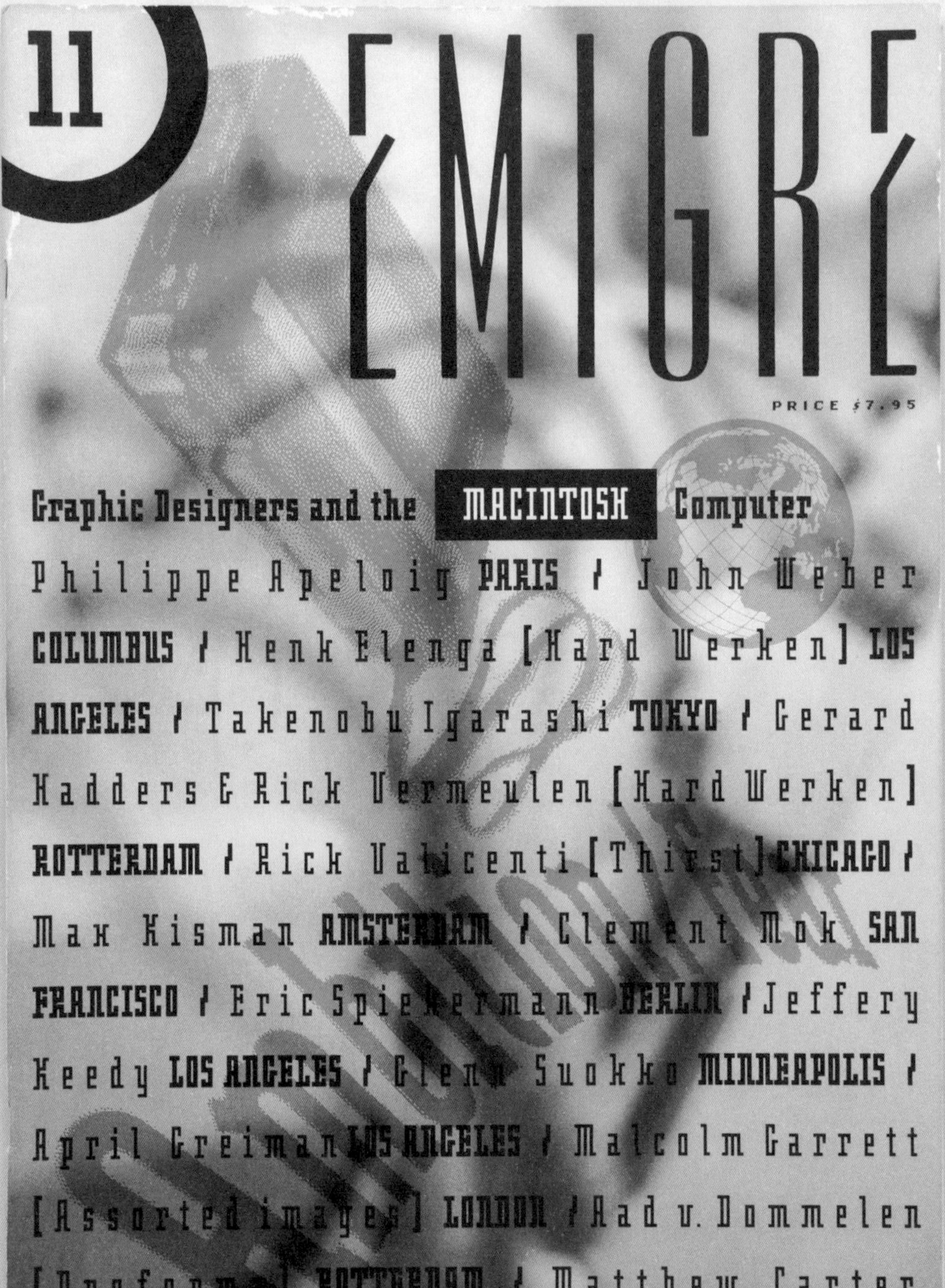

11

EMIGRE

PRICE $7.95

Graphic Designers and the MACINTOSH Computer

Philippe Apeloig PARIS / John Weber COLUMBUS / Henk Elenga [Hard Werken] LOS ANGELES / Takenobu Igarashi TOKYO / Gerard Hadders & Rick Vermeulen [Hard Werken] ROTTERDAM / Rick Valicenti [Thirst] CHICAGO / Max Kisman AMSTERDAM / Clement Mok SAN FRANCISCO / Eric Spiekermann BERLIN / Jeffery Keedy LOS ANGELES / Glenn Suokko MINNEAPOLIS / April Greiman LOS ANGELES / Malcolm Garrett [Assorted images] LONDON / Aad v. Dommelen [Proforma] ROTTERDAM / Matthew Carter BOSTON

Emigre
Country: USA

Design: Rudy VanderLans
Fonts: Zuzana Licko

re.designing stereotypes

Emigre #13. Price $7.95

Emigre
Country: USA

Design: Rudy VanderLans
Fonts: Zuzana Licko

THE ARCHITECTS' JOURNAL

AJ

7 MARCH 1990/£1.10

NEWS/Cambridge poser for Terry

Civic trust to 'sell' logo

FEATURE/The Waverley Challenge

BUILDINGS/High school craft

PRACTICE/New Copyright Act

AJ (Architects' Journal)
Country: UK

Design: unidentified

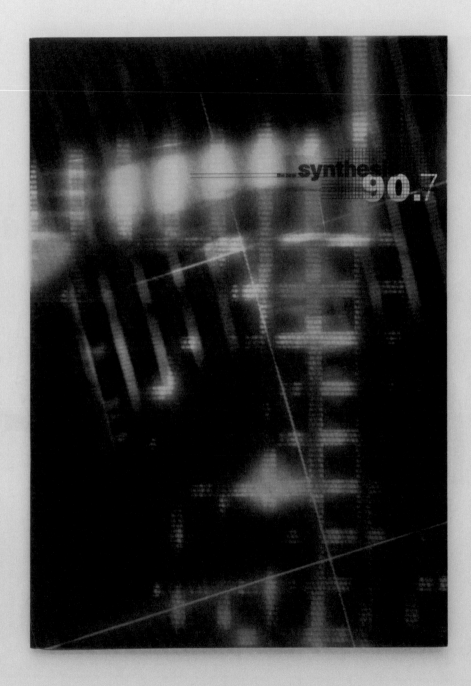

Eye
Country: UK

Cover: Detail from Het Boek
van PTT, Piet Zwart 1930–38
Art Director: Stephen Coates

Emigre
Country: USA

Design: Rudy VanderLans
Fonts: Zuzana Licko

december 1990   Hfl. 15 / Bfr. 270

Tijdschrift voor architectuur

Oase 28 over **Snelheid en zwaarte** Wim Nijenhuis → De passie van het hiaat / Willem Heesen & Wilfried van Winden → Het landschap van de Reichsautobahnen / Erik Terlouw → Image building / De Nijl → Laagbouw in hoge dichtheid / Giorgio Grassi → Een mening over het onderwijs en de voorwaarden van ons werk

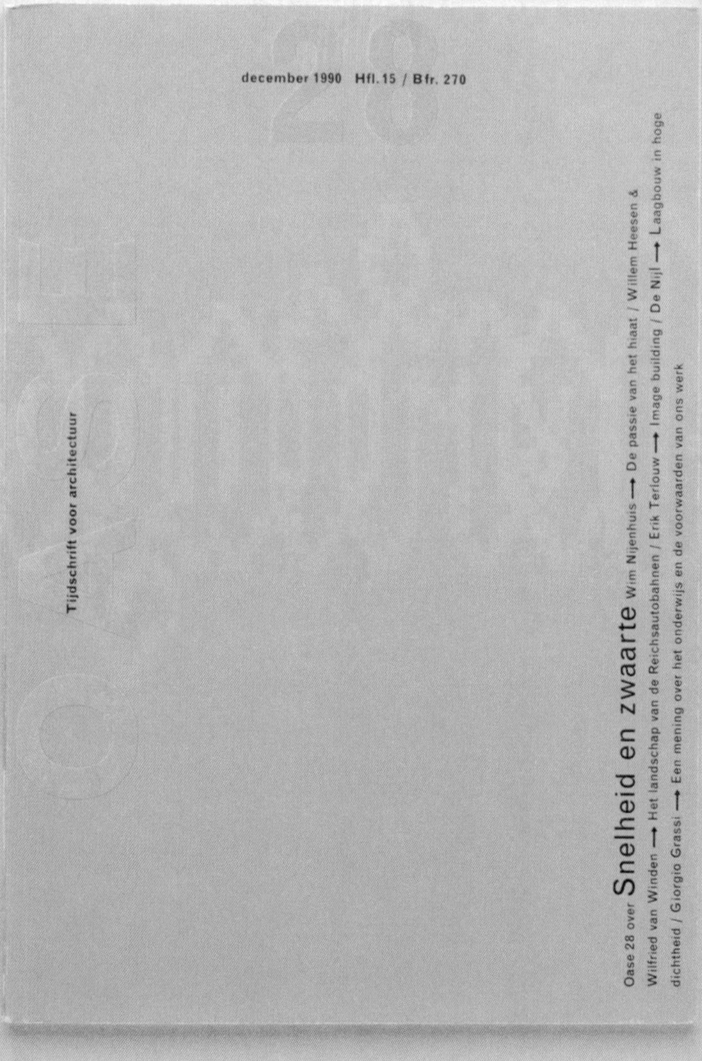

OASE Journal for Architecture
Country: Netherlands

Cover Design: Karel Martens

SOUND DES!GN !!!

ISSUE SIXTEEN

PRICE - $7.95

EMIGRE

Emigre
Country: USA

Design: Rudy VanderLans
Fonts: Zuzana Licko

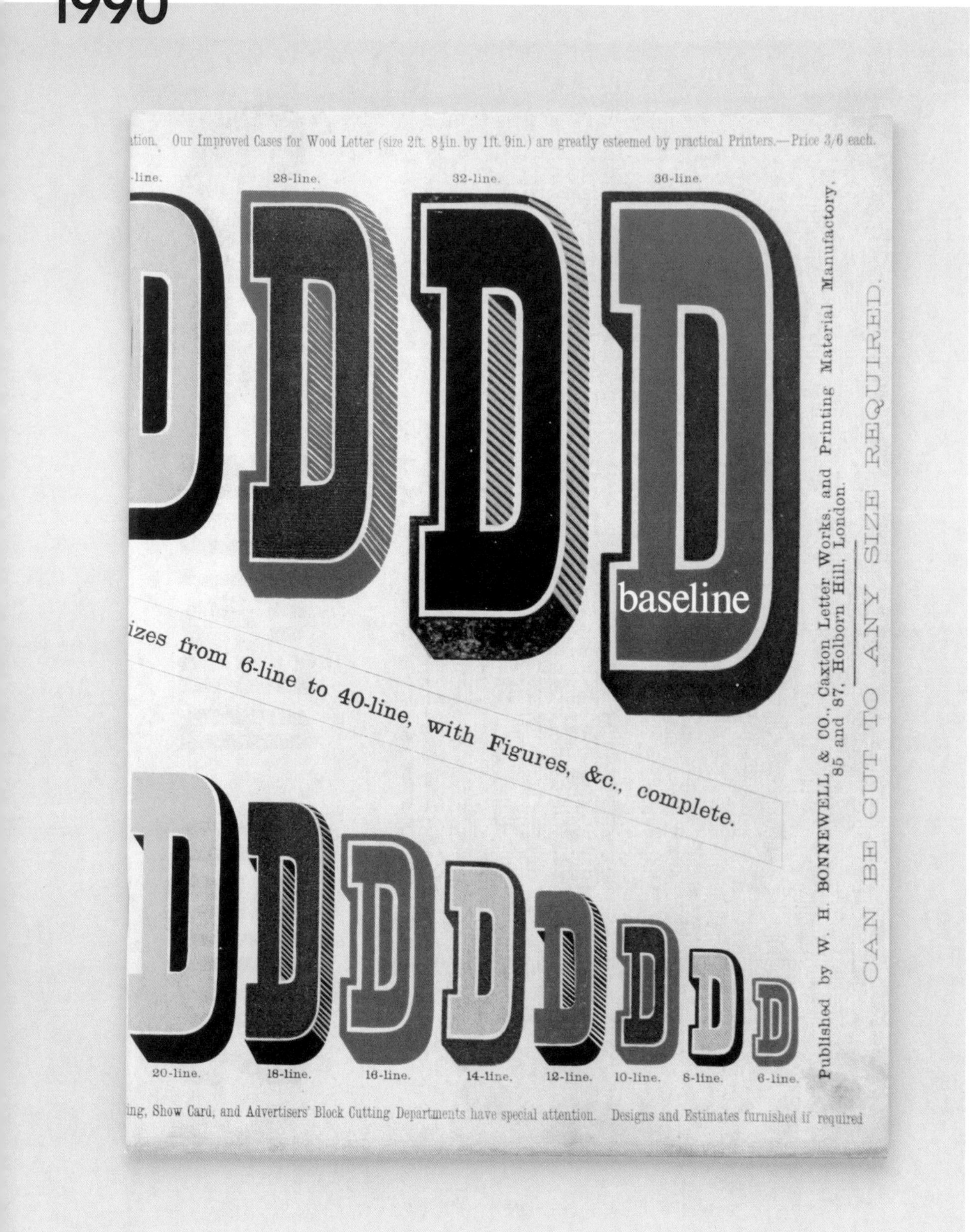

Our Improved Cases for Wood Letter (size 2ft. 8½in. by 1ft. 9in.) are greatly esteemed by practical Printers.—Price 3/6 each.
28-line.
32-line.
36-line.
baseline
izes from 6-line to 40-line, with Figures, &c., complete.
20-line.
18-line.
16-line.
14-line.
12-line.
10-line.
8-line.
6-line.
ing, Show Card, and Advertisers' Block Cutting Departments have special attention. Designs and Estimates furnished if required
Published by W. H. BONNEWELL & CO., Caxton Letter Works, and Printing Material Manufactory,
85 and 87, Holborn Hill, London.
CAN BE CUT TO ANY SIZE REQUIRED.

Baseline
Country: UK

Type specimen: 'Wood type'
by W. H. Bonwell
Design: Newell & Sorrell

Emigre
Country: USA

Design: Rudy VanderLans
Fonts: Zuzana Licko

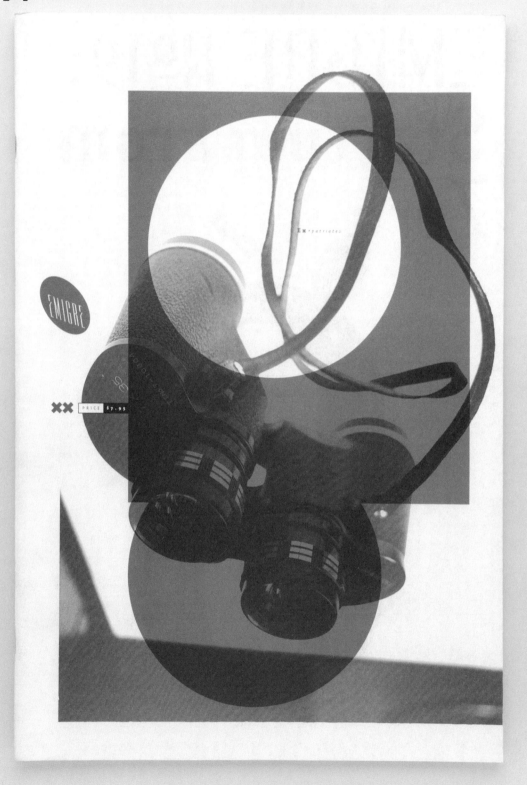

Emigre
Country: USA

Design: Rudy VanderLans
Fonts: Zuzana Licko

Redactioneel De moderne architectuur heeft het vraagstuk van de
vorm altijd trachten te omzeilen. Idealiter zou de vorm als
vanzelf moeten voortkomen uit een of ander proces, als het
zuiver logistieke resultaat van een aantal factoren, of als een
wat duistere intuïtie van autonome voortgang die zich
uitkristalliseert in een soort momentopname. In de plattegrond levert dit niet direct problemen op; de scheidingen
en verbindingen binnen dit horizontale vlak laten zich veelal
gemakkelijk lezen als een directe uitdrukking van een aantal
interne relaties. Anders ligt het in het verticale vlak, met
name aan de buitenzijde. Zoals Joost Meuwissen stelt in zijn
in deze OASE afgedrukte artikel: 'Van boven ziet het er
allemaal nog wel aardig uit, in de plattegrond. Maar van
voren beginnen de problemen.' Een proces heeft geen
buitenkant. Aan een proces kun je niet vragen welke positie
het inneemt binnen een (historisch gegroeide) maatschappelijke constellatie; je kunt niet vragen waar het proces voor
'staat', je kunt alleen maar vragen of het 'werkt'. Het is
vermoedelijk vooral hierdoor dat de moderne architectuur
neigt naar een transparantie, die de motoriek van het proces
min of meer volgens het model van het aquarium poogt te
veraanschouwelijken of, wanneer we het begrip 'modern'
niet al te nauw definiëren, naar een gebruik van het gevelvlak als 'bill-board', als een soort reclamepaneel waarop los
van het eigenlijke gebouw tekens worden aangebracht. De
door het gebouw opgeroepen beelden zouden, in dit laatste
geval, als tekens mee moeten rouleren in de stedelijke
communicatie, maar krijgen juist doordat ze worden bevrijd
van elke consequentie, van elke binding aan een structuur,
nooit een werkelijke (maatschappelijke, algemene) betekenis.

   In de moderne architectonische handboeken en
voorbeeldenboeken gaat de aandacht dan ook vrijwel volledig uit naar de plattegrond. Anders dan in de leerboeken uit
de renaissance en het classicisme ontbreekt een uiteenzetting
van de tektonische middelen waarmee de opstand van het
gevelvlak als architectonisch ontwerp zou kunnen worden
opgebouwd vrijwel volledig. Toch moet, natuurlijk, elk
architectonisch ontwerp uiteindelijk een precieze vorm
krijgen, ook aan de buitenzijde. Le Corbusier is een van de
weinige moderne architecten die zich welbewust en expliciet
hebben beziggehouden met de vorm van de opstand; eerst

Oase N° 31 over de tektoniek van de opstand & Aldo Rossi's plan voor het Bonnefantenmuseum

Tijdschrift voor architectuur   december 1991   Hfl 15 / Bfr 270

calarts calarts calarts
california institute of the arts california institute of the arts california institute of the arts california institut

new faces new faces new faces

EMIGRE

$7.95 $7.95 $7.95
issue #21 issue #21 issue # 21 issue #21 issue #21

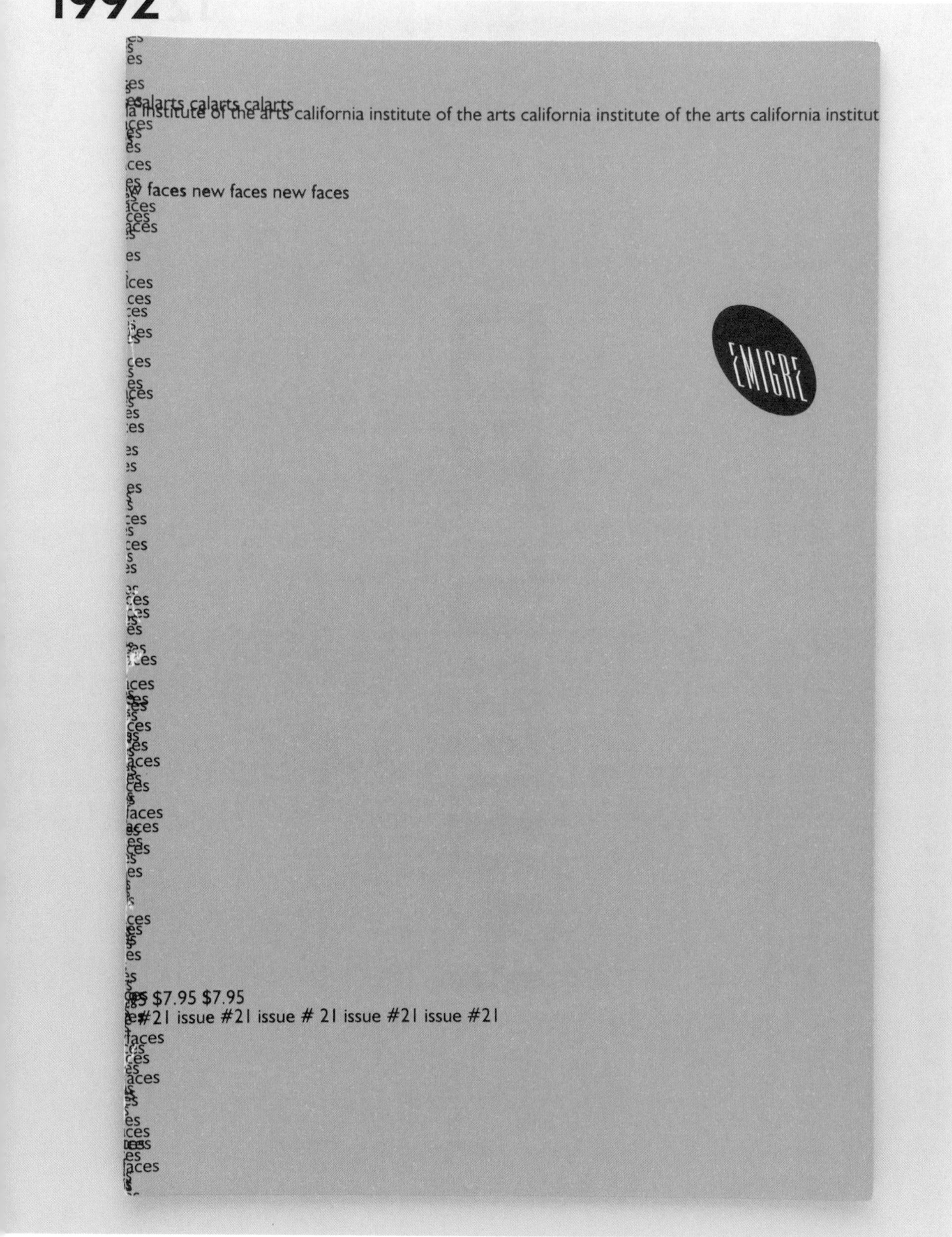

Emigre
Country: USA

Design: Rudy VanderLans
Fonts: Zuzana Licko

Emigre No. 22. Price $7.95

ck Bell Ni

"Teach"

Nick Bell and the London College of Printing.

Emigre
Country: USA

Design: Rudy VanderLans
Fonts: Zuzana Licko

Emigre
Country: USA

Design: Rudy VanderLans
Fonts: Zuzana Licko

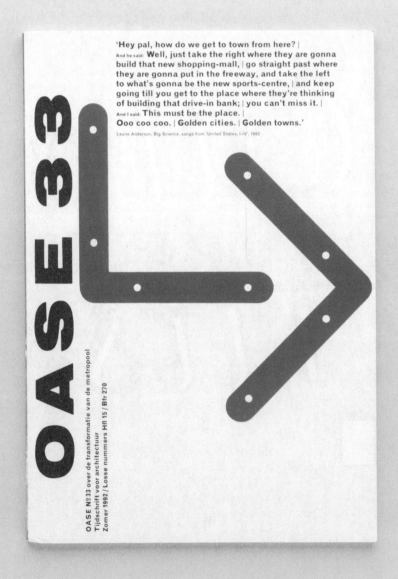

OASE Journal for Architecture
Country: Netherlands

Cover Design: Karel Martens

neo-
mania

Nº 24

Price$7.95

Tijdschrift voor architectuur   Herfst 1992   Hfl 15 / Bfr 270
OASE Nº 34 over het interieur / Gaston Bachelard **De hoeken** /
Frans Sturkenboom **Het dierenhol** / Pieter Jan Gijsberts / **Een transparante**
fantasmagorie & **Inundatie van de blik** / Wilfried van Winden **Materie**
en maskerade / Willemijn Wilms Floet **Architecture on the rocks** /
Michiel Riedijk **Raster, labyrint en grot**

OASE Journal for Architecture
Country: Netherlands   Cover Design: Karel Martens

Baseline
Country: UK

'Van Morrison' cover: Wes Wilson
Design: Lippa Pearce Design

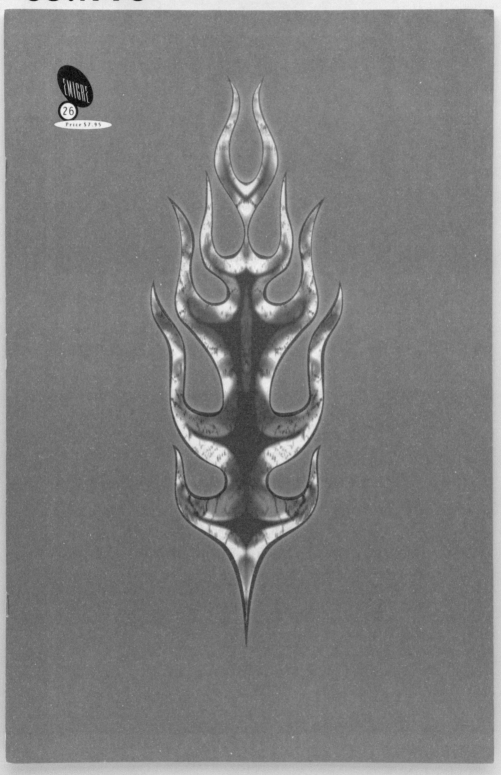

Emigre
Country: USA

Design: Rudy VanderLans
Fonts: Zuzana Licko

Fuse
Country: UK

Design: Neville Brody,
Jon Wozencroft, John Critchley

$7.95   issue # 27.

+ David Carson

EMIGRE

Emigre
Country: USA

Design: Rudy VanderLans
Fonts: Zuzana Licko

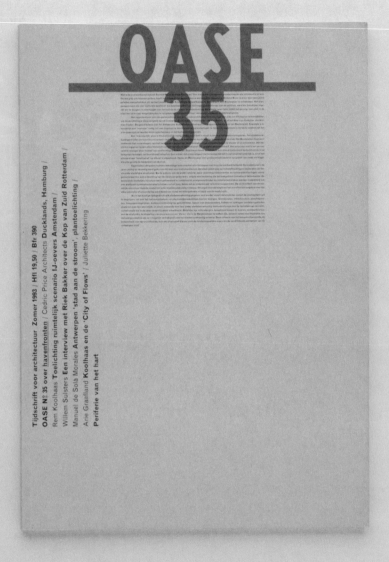

Cover Design:
Karel Martens, Roger Willems

Emigre
Country: USA

Design: Rudy VanderLans
Fonts: Zuzana Licko

THE INTERNATIONAL REVIEW OF GRAPHIC DESIGN   No.9   VOL. 3 1993

PRINTED IN GREAT BRITAIN

eye

Eye
Country: UK

Art Direction: Stephen Coates
Cover image: Roman Cieslewicz,
taken from Opus magazine, 1968

FORM+ZWECK 78 1993 ZEITSCHRIFT FÜR GESTALTUNG

Form+Zweck
Country: Germany

Cover Design: cyan

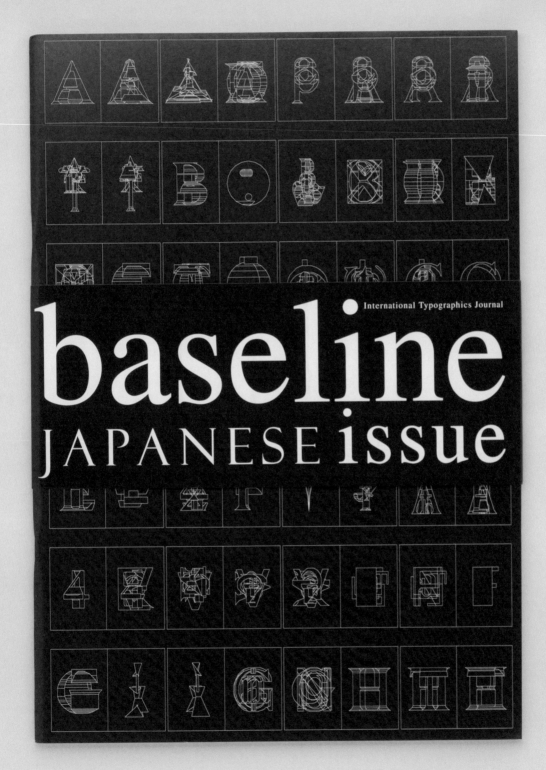

International Typographics Journal

baseline
JAPANESE issue

Baseline
Country: UK

'Computer Art', letter shape designs:
Hâjime Tachibana
Design: Lippa Pearce Design

143

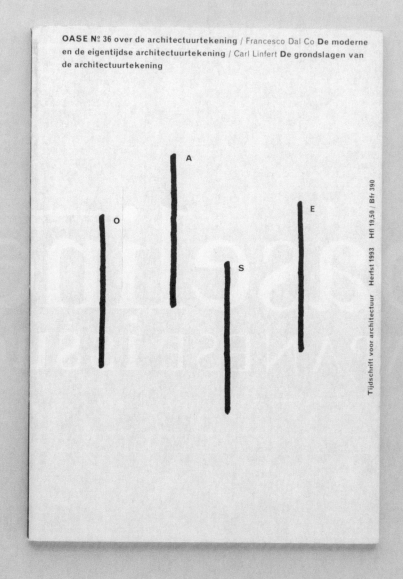

OASE N° 36 over de architectuurtekening / Francesco Dal Co De moderne en de eigentijdse architectuurtekening / Carl Linfert De grondslagen van de architectuurtekening

O A S E

Tijdschrift voor architectuur   Herfst 1993   Hfl 19,50 / Bfr 390

OASE Journal for Architecture
Country: Netherlands   Cover Design: Karel Martens

numéro 9/10 octobre 1993

signes

70 francs

Signes
Country: France

Cover Design: Muriel Paris

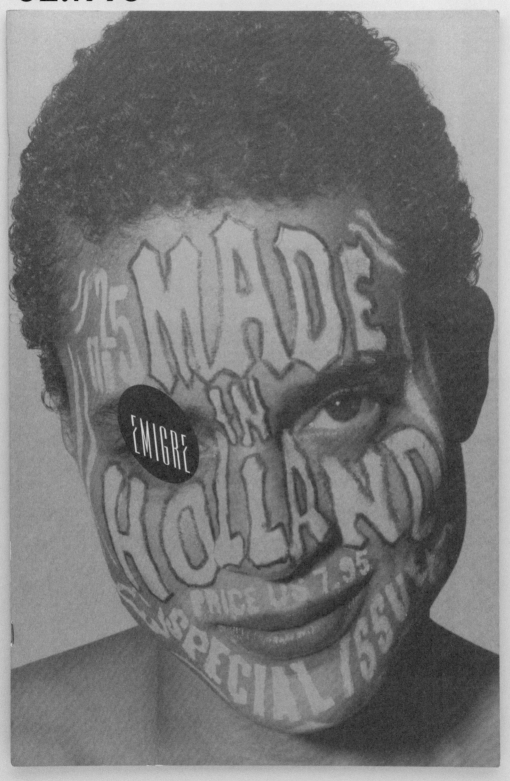

Emigre
Country: USA

Art Direction: Vincent van Baar,
Armand Mevis

Да!
Русский журнал
для дизайнеров-графиков
№1 1994

Da!
Country: Russia   Cover Design: Vladimir Krichevski

Tijdschrift voor architectuur Het wereldontwerp
Michiel Riedijk Het wereldontwerp / Erik Terlouw De grenzen van de tuin /
Robert-Jan van Pelt Mens en kosmos in Huygens' Hofwijck /
Pieter van Wesemael Mundaneum en Cité Mondiale /
Karel Teige Mundaneum / Le Corbusier Ter verdediging van de architectuur /
Richard Buckminster Fuller Het wereldspel – Hoe laten we de wereld werken /
Jurjen Zeinstra Het wereldbewustzijn van Richard Buckminster Fuller

OASE 41

OASE Journal for Architecture
Country: Netherlands

Cover Design:
Karel Martens, Roger Willems

Emigre
Country: USA

Cover Design:
The Designers Republic

Emigre

No. 32

price $7.95

Emigre
Country: USA

Cover Design: Rudy VanderLans

Form+Zweck
Country: Germany

Cover Design: cyan

Emigre
Country: USA

Design: Rudy VanderLans
Fonts: Zuzana Licko

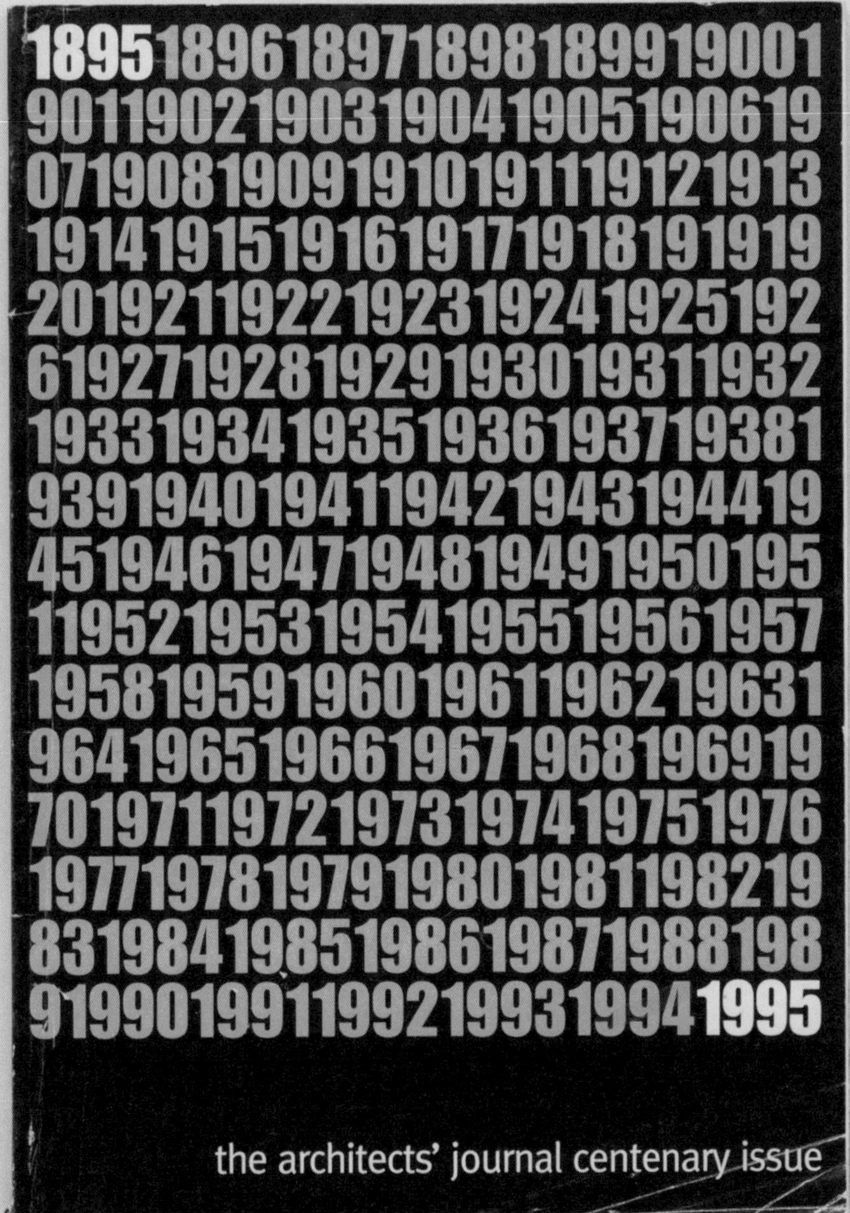

1895 1896 1897 1898 1899 1900 1901 1902 1903 1904 1905 1906 1907 1908 1909 1910 1911 1912 1913 1914 1915 1916 1917 1918 1919 1920 1921 1922 1923 1924 1925 1926 1927 1928 1929 1930 1931 1932 1933 1934 1935 1936 1937 1938 1939 1940 1941 1942 1943 1944 1945 1946 1947 1948 1949 1950 1951 1952 1953 1954 1955 1956 1957 1958 1959 1960 1961 1962 1963 1964 1965 1966 1967 1968 1969 1970 1971 1972 1973 1974 1975 1976 1977 1978 1979 1980 1981 1982 1983 1984 1985 1986 1987 1988 1989 1990 1991 1992 1993 1994 **1995**

the architects' journal centenary issue

Da!
Country: Russia

Cover Design: Vladimir Krichevski

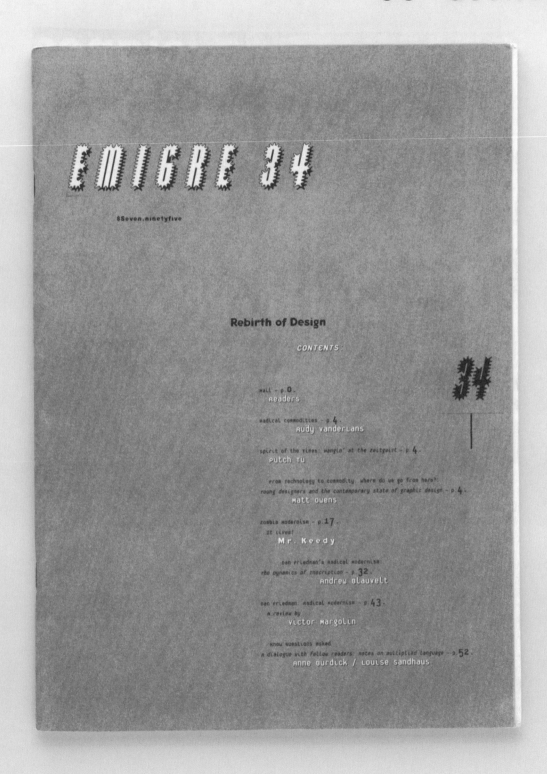

EMIGRE 34

$Seven.ninetyfive

Rebirth of Design

CONTENTS

Emigre
Country: USA

Design: Rudy VanderLans
Fonts: Zuzana Licko

Signes
Country: France

Cover Design: Alex Jordan

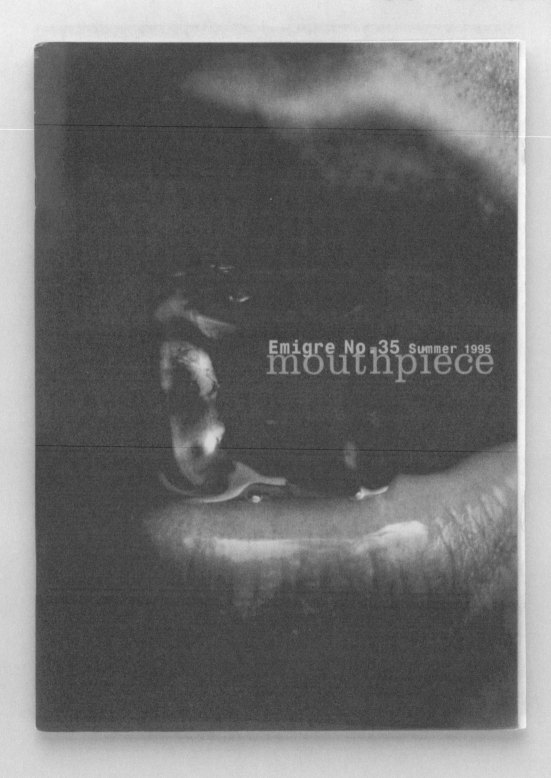

Emigre No. 35 Summer 1995
mouthpiece

Emigre
Country: USA

Cover Design: Anne Burdick

Hard Werken
Country: Netherlands

Cover Design: Hard Werken Studio

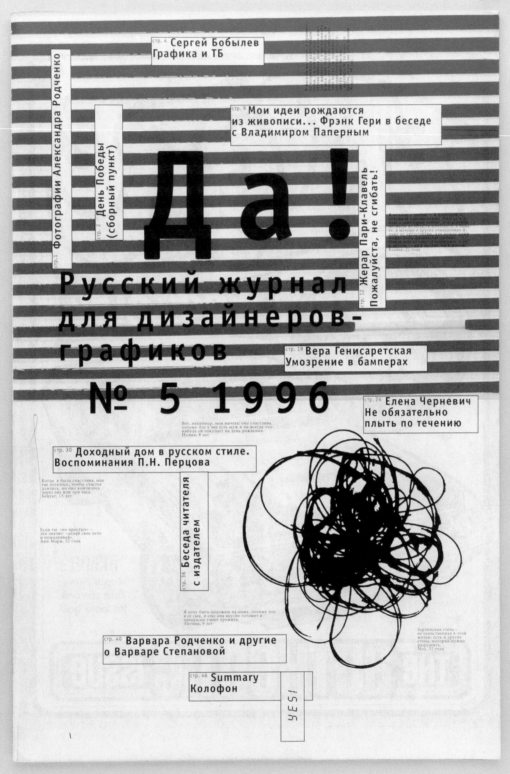

стр. 1 Фотографии Александра Родченко

стр. 2 День Победы (сборный пункт)

стр. 4 Сергей Бобылев
Графика и ТБ

стр. 9 Мои идеи рождаются из живописи... Фрэнк Гери в беседе с Владимиром Паперным

стр. 12 Жерар Пари-Клавель
Пожалуйста, не сгибать!

Да!

Русский журнал для дизайнеров-графиков

№ 5 1996

стр. 19 Вера Генисаретская
Умозрение в бамперах

стр. 24 Елена Черневич
Не обязательно плыть по течению

стр. 30 Доходный дом в русском стиле.
Воспоминания П.Н. Перцова

стр. 36 Беседа читателя с издателем

стр. 40 Варвара Родченко и другие о Варваре Степановой

стр. 46 Summary
Колофон

Emigre
Country: USA

Design: Rudy VanderLans
Fonts: Zuzana Licko

Fuse
Country: UK

Design: Neville Brody,
Jon Wozencroft, Tom Hingston

Emigre
Country: USA

Design: Rudy VanderLans
Fonts: Zuzana Licko

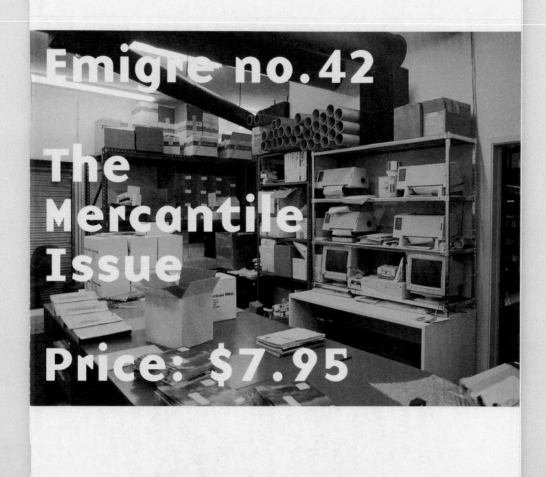

Emigre no.42

The Mercantile Issue

Price: $7.95

Emigre
Country: USA

Design: Rudy VanderLans
Fonts: Zuzana Licko

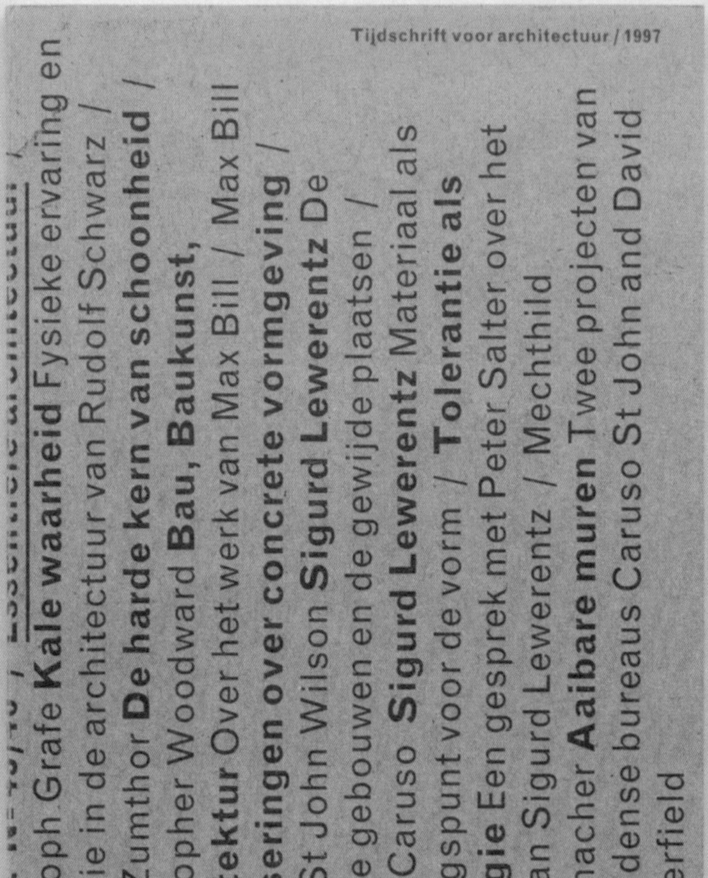

Tijdschrift voor architectuur / 1997

Christoph Grafe **Kale waarheid** Fysieke ervaring en essentie in de architectuur van Rudolf Schwarz / Peter Zumthor **De harde kern van schoonheid** / Christopher Woodward **Bau, Baukunst, Architektur** Over het werk van Max Bill / Max Bill **Preciseringen over concrete vormgeving** / Colin St John Wilson **Sigurd Lewerentz** De gewijde gebouwen en de gewijde plaatsen / Adam Caruso **Sigurd Lewerentz** Materiaal als uitgangspunt voor de vorm / **Tolerantie als strategie** Een gesprek met Peter Salter over het werk van Sigurd Lewerentz / Mechthild Stuhlmacher **Aaibare muren** Twee projecten van de Londense bureaus Caruso St John and David Chipperfield

OASE Journal for Architecture
Country: Netherlands
Cover Design: Karel Martens

Emigre no.47 $7.95

Relocating

Design

Summer 1998

TYP (Typografisch Papier)
Country: Netherlands

Cover Design: Max Kisman

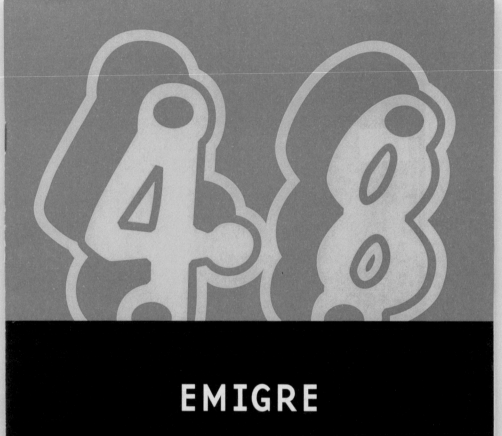

Emigre
Country: USA

Design: Rudy VanderLans
Fonts: Zuzana Licko

Design Issues
Country: USA

Cover Design: Ken Hiebert

baSeline

international typographics magazine

c7c panair do bras

baseline is the authoritative and informative magazine about type and typography, within graphics and the visual arts. Published three times a year, baseline is internationally recognized for its contributors, contents and award-winning design, which range from tradition to experiment.

Issue 27 1999 UK £11.00 Printed in England www.baselinemagazine.com

The work of Mary Viera	Prof Friedrich Friedl
Notgeld from Neustadt	Jilly and Ian McLaren
Paul Rand's laboratory	Steven Heller
Lines of movement	David Gibson
Hans Schleger – starting from zero	Hans Dieter Reichert
Phill Grimshaw – a character study	Max Dunes

Baseline
Country: UK

Cover image: Mary Viera
(dc7c panair do brazil)
Design: HDR design

GRAPHIC DESIGN INCL.

EMIGRE No.53 / WINTER 2000 / PRICE 7.95

Emigre
Country: USA

Design: Rudy VanderLans
Fonts: Zuzana Licko

typ

Circular

Magazine
of the
Typographic
Circle

Circular
Country: UK

Cover Design: Lippa Pearce

MAY 2000 £4.25 UK / $10.95 US A CENTAUR PUBLICATION

Creative Review
Country: UK

Art Director: Nathan Gale

Interview: Patrick Burgoyne

Q You have been editor of *Creative Review* (1981–present, UK) for a number of years – what are the biggest changes that you have navigated through in your time as editor?

A The Internet turned the business of publishing magazines upside down. Pre-digital, magazines enjoyed a very simple, very profitable model – identify an audience, understand it, build it, bring it together and sell access to it. Suddenly, much of what magazines had the exclusive ability to deliver – helping people find a job, giving them access to information, giving brands access to their consumers en masse – could be done quicker, cheaper and often better online. Who wouldn't want to post a job vacancy online for free where millions could potentially see it instead of paying a magazine hundreds of pounds to run a print ad?

For years, magazines put their faith in the idea that an alternative model would replace the old one – it would be iPad apps, or digital subscriptions, events, free circulation – now, we are told, the new model is that there is no model. To an extent that's true: we all have to pick and choose which of the many options open to us work for our particular audiences and brands. All magazines have had to do a lot of soul-searching, asking themselves what they really stand for, what value they actually have and how best to deliver it. Though painful, that has been very healthy. Magazines have had to up their game.

Q What are the challenges of designing a publication for a design-savvy audience?

A I've always thought there are two ways you can go – try and be as innovative and exciting with the editorial design of the publication as the work you are trying to show, or step back, keep things simple, and let the work you are showcasing be the star. On *CR* we have always tried to do the latter. In part this is for practical reasons – we have a very limited budget and just one art director – the brilliant Paul Pensom – to do everything. Extremely complex layouts requiring many hours' bespoke work are not really an option. But also, from a philosophical standpoint, I always thought it important to respect the work, not to crop it or overlay it, to let it be seen in as pure a way as possible. That's how I'd like to see my work treated.

Q How are *Creative Review* covers decided?

A With our Annuals, we can work a long time in advance and commission out the covers. This has led to some great imagery, with people like Craig Ward, Morag Myerscough and, last year, Warren du Preez and Nick Thornton Jones, producing amazing covers for us with – importantly in these days of social media – fascinating backstories to tell. With other covers, we do still commission some original imagery – when budgets allow and if we don't have anything suitable from the images we are featuring on the inside pages. At other times, we will use something by one of the people we are covering inside. Then it's a case of lots of discussion between Paul and me, and often the rest of the editorial team. We will usually get three or four versions proofed, sometimes with completely different images, and put them up on the wall. If we have time and resources we might talk about using a finish to bring out a particular element – a foil or a varnish, maybe – or we might use a different cover stock. Sometimes suppliers approach us to see if we want to showcase some new production technique for them. But it's really a process of trial and error and lots of conversations. And, for me, it remains one of the most enjoyable parts of the job.

Q What current design publications from around the world do you admire?

A It's not really a design title, though it is very design aware, but I really admire the world that *Monocle* (2007–present, UK) has built, and the way in which they can bring in commercial partners without it feeling jarring or inappropriate. The revival of Monotype's *The Recorder* (2014–present, UK) is beautifully done. And *Kyoorius Magazine* (2006–present, India) is doing great job in showcasing and nurturing the Indian graphic design scene.

Creative Review
1981—present
UK

Creative Review
1981—present
UK

Q Designers, journalists, educators and publishers seem to be agreed that print is making a comeback. It seems print's demise was predicted prematurely? Where do you stand on this question?

A If you go into any half-decent newsagent you will see an incredible array of magazines today. Jeremy Leslie's excellent magCulture project – with blog, shop and events – has done a fantastic job in documenting and nurturing this apparent print revival. But, like vinyl, the nature of print publishing has changed. Very few of those beautifully produced magazines in the newsagent will be making any money for the people involved. A lot of them are done for love, which shows in the high production values and evident care taken over every page. But it also means that very few of those contributing to the magazines – the writers, photographers and illustrators – are getting paid. A lot of titles are a means to an end – they might act as a branding device or a way to create a presence, while the real money is made in events or in other areas. Or they might be about demonstrating a love for, or expertise in, a particular field in the hope that paying partners will commission the team behind them for advertising or other work. Many will burn bright for a few issues and then just disappear. It's fantastic that so many people still see print magazines as an exciting medium through which to say what they want to say to the world. The magazines that endure will be those that make meaningful connections with their audiences and do so in a way that cannot be replicated or bettered online.

Patrick Burgoyne started his career at Creative Review as a staff writer and has been editor since 1999. He has authored several books on design and visual culture.

**Creative Review
1981—present
UK**

**Creative Review
1981—present
UK**

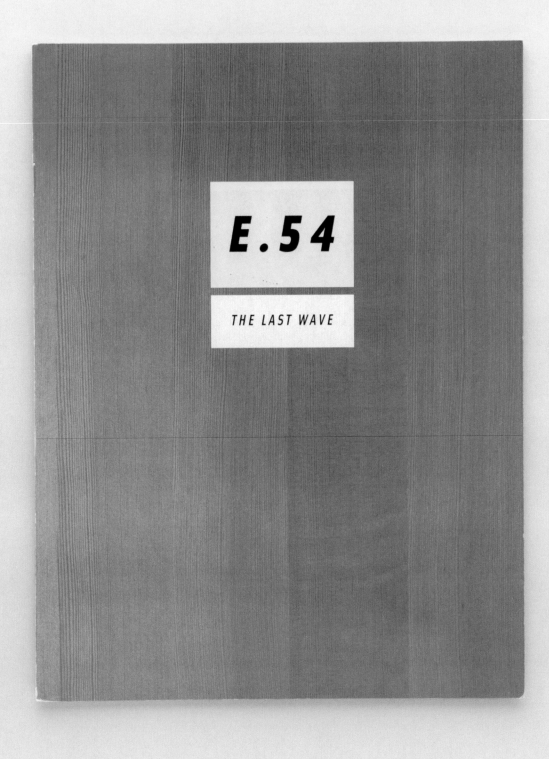

Emigre
Country: USA

Design: Rudy VanderLans
Fonts: Zuzana Licko

Emigre No. 55

The leisure time issue
Summer 2000

Price: seven.ninetyfive

Emigre
Country: USA

Design: Rudy VanderLans
Fonts: Zuzana Licko

Idea
Country: Japan

Cover Design:
Charles S Anderson Design Co.

Idea
Country: Japan

Cover Design: Blue Source

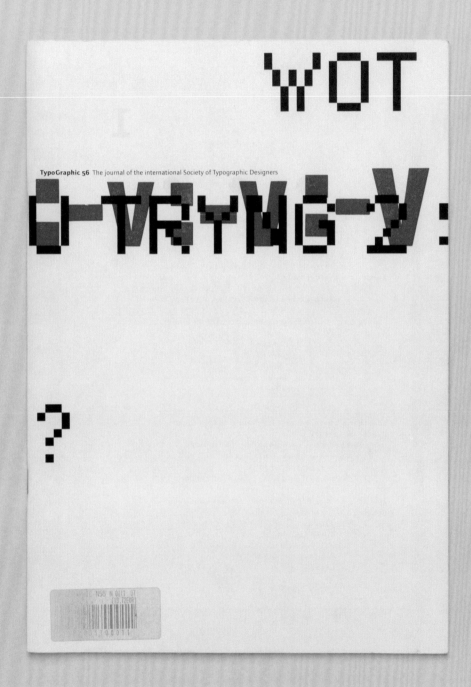

TypoGraphic 56 The journal of the international Society of Typographic Designers

1

● ● ●

Why another graphic design magazine?

This pilot issue of ...
          (a graphic design / visual culture magazine)
hopes to answer itself
          being an encyclopaedia of previous attempts
          with extended articles on a select few

During this field trip we hope to plot the next issue
          i.e.   how?
                    where?
                    when?
                    who?
          based on the experiences of those who
          tried already

Those 3 dots were chosen as the title for being
something close to an internationally-recognised
typographic mark
but now they seem even more appropriate as
a representation of what we intend the project to become:
          A magazine in flux
          ready to adjust itself to content

and here is the first list of our aims to date:
(to be)   critical
          flexible
          international
          portfolio-free
          rigorous
          useful

Dot Dot Dot
Country: UK/Netherlands   Cover Design: Dot Dot Dot

Adbusters
Country: Canada

Art Director: Barnbrook

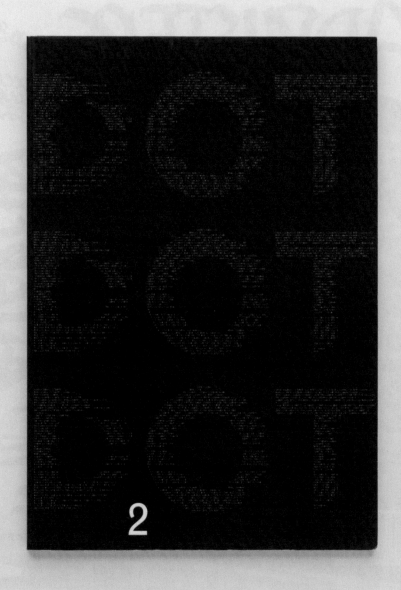

2

Dot Dot Dot
Country: UK/Netherlands

Cover Design: Dot Dot Dot

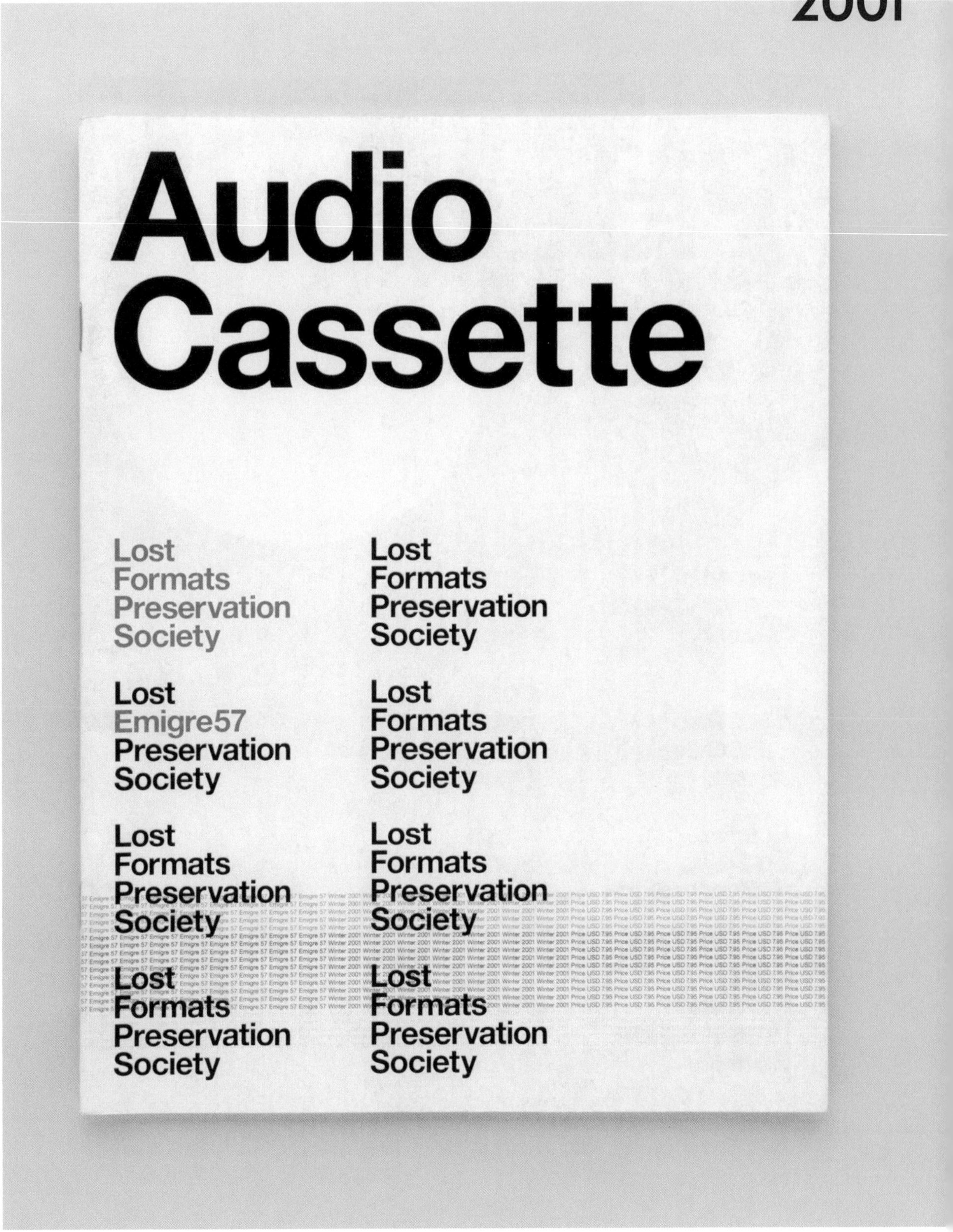

Audio Cassette

Lost
Formats
Preservation
Society

Lost
Emigre57
Preservation
Society

Lost
Formats
Preservation
Society

Lost
Formats
Preservation
Society

Lost
Formats
Preservation
Society

Lost
Formats
Preservation
Society

Lost
Formats
Preservation
Society

Lost
Formats
Preservation
Society

Baseline
Country: UK

Cover Design: Siegfried Odermatt

Q *Baseline* (1979–present, UK) covers usually came with a wrap-around poster or bellyband – what was your thinking?

A I inherited the bellyband from the time when *Baseline* was published by Letraset and designed by Domenic Lippa at Newell and Sorrell. The general idea of the bellyband is that it seals the magazine, to give it a kind of exclusive and novelty feel. From issue 10 to 16 it carried the title in lowercase (Times New Roman) and the theme of the particular issue: No.10, Cassandre (1988); No.11, Bradbury Thompson (1989); No.12, St Bride's (1990); No.13, Bodoni (1990); No.14, Sans Serif (1991); No.15, Psychedelic (1992); No.16, Japanese (1993).

I became involved with No.17 in 1994, and used a transparent bellyband featuring only the name, *Baseline – International Typographic Journal*, in a number of various typefaces for each letter. The transparent paper of the bellyband for No.17 was used to integrate with the cover. From No.18 until No.24 we kept the bellyband and produced it in contrasting colours and different materials (uncoated and coated paper) and made more of a feature of it. With No.25 we changed the bellyband, gave it slightly different proportions and added the contents of the magazine.

In 1998, for No.26, we added a jacket to the magazine. This was to introduce an additional medium and give the magazine a more exclusive feel. The jacket also doubled up as a poster (production marks, printing and registration marks were part of the format). In the United States, the magazine was sold without the jacket.

Also, the bellyband became a bookmark and was inserted vertically between cover and magazine in the top left-hand corner. The advantage of that position was that the title was better identifiable on the magazine racks. The previous bellyband, which was wrapped around the centre of the cover, was always partly hidden. With the redesign of issue No.52 in 2007 we also looked at the design and position of the jacket in relation to the cover. A different way of folding resulted in a shorter appearance and revealed the cover with its title and content list. The bookmark and previous bellyband were redundant, and the design was more robust.

Q Do the designers of design magazines have it easy? After all, they have a design-literate audience. Or is it the opposite – designers are famously critical and therefore hard to please?

A I would think designers of design magazines have a special responsibility to work to a high standard when designing for their peers. Part of the responsibility is to find the right balance between expression and restraint (to show the work of your colleagues), but also to build a relationship with the author and the contents of the article. At *Baseline* we work with a 12-column grid, which allows us to create individual visual interpretations and careful designs for the various articles. An eye for detail is essential not just for the layout, but also in the print production because, for example, different over-printed colours create different moods and effects. Small reversed-out type and line work out of big solid colour areas are very sensitive and need special detailed attention.

Q When you took on the design of *Baseline*, who and what were your main inspirations?

A My inspirations have always been Jan Tschichold, Willy Fleckhaus, Anthony Froshaug and Brian Grimbly. Later, Otl Aicher and Helmut Schmid. At the time of taking on *Baseline* my inspirations were Alan Fletcher and Ken Garland. General inspirations are good old work ethics and professional reliability: don't let the client down (in the case of *Baseline* the client was Letraset). Further on I realised the educational potential of *Baseline* – to inform the reader about important 'classical' and 'contemporary' subjects.

Q Do you have some favourite *Baseline* covers?

A No.29, with a jacket by Alan Kitching; No.30, with a jacket by HDR Visual Communication (using packaging by Helmut Schmid). No.40 and No.62, both with jackets by HDR Visual Communication.

Baseline
1979–present
UK

Q Do you have a favourite cover for a design magazine – past or present?

A From the past: *ulm* (1958); *Bauen+Wohnen* (1952); *Neue Grafik* (1958); *Abitare*, 297 (1991); *Domus* (1928); and *Frankfurter Allgemeine Magazin* (dates unknown). From the present: *Typography Today*, special number; *Inventario* 11 (2015); *Eye* (1990–present, UK).

Hans Dieter Reichert is a leading designer, art director and publisher and has edited and art-directed Baseline *since 1995.*

ulm
1958—68
Germany

Neue Grafik
1958—65
Switzerland

INTERNATIONAL ISSUE
GERMAN / ENGLISH

ISSN 1438-1753   B 3149   8,60 €
www.novumnet.de

novum

WORLD OF GRAPHIC DESIGN 01/02

0,000 000 000 324

Diese Dezimalzahl ergibt sich, wenn man die Zahl 2 durch die derzeitige Weltbevölkerung teilt. Sie ist somit die rechnerische Größe von zwei Personen auf der Erde.* / This decimal number comes from dividing 2 by the current figure for the world's population. It is thus a mathematical representation of two people on Earth.*

■ **karlssonwilker**
Design pur aus NY
Pure design enjoyment from NY

■ **Kilmer & Kilmer**
Werbestrategen & Markenmacher
Advertising strategists and brand-makers

■ **Sylvia Neuner**
Faszination Illustration
Fascination of illustration

novum PLUS **KOSMETIK / COSMETICS**

Idea
Country: Japan

Cover Design: Masayoshi Nakajo

Eye
Country: UK

Art Direction and Cover Art:
Nick Bell

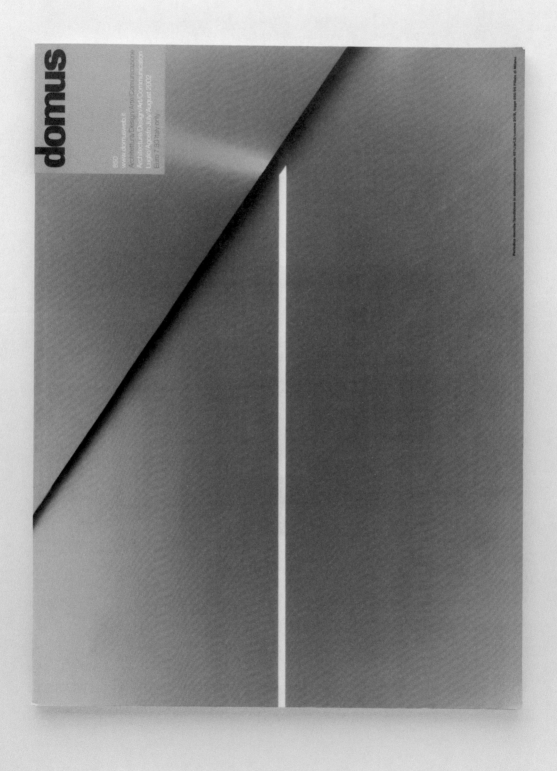

Domus
Country: Italy

Creative Director: Simon Esterson

Dot dot dot Nº4 (ISSN 1615-1968)
a. Archæological æsthetics b. Based on true stories c. Stroppy/Revelatory

Dot Dot Dot
Country: UK/Netherlands

Cover Design: Dot Dot Dot

OASE Journal for Architecture
Country: Netherlands

Cover Director:
Hans Gremmen, Karel Martens,
Werkplaats Typografie

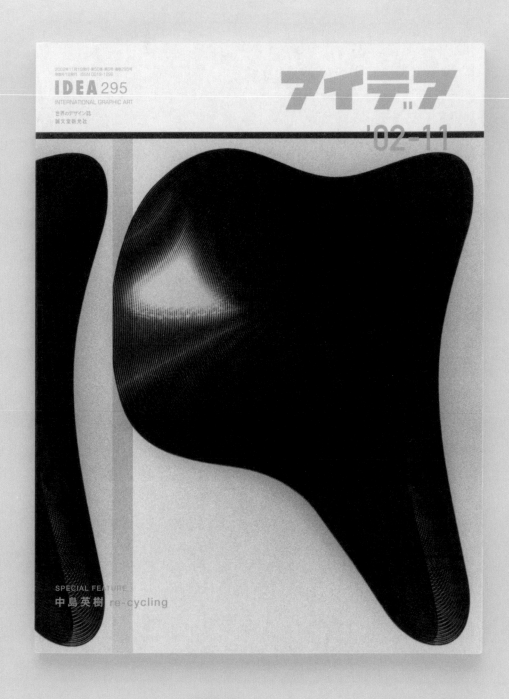

TYPOGRAPHIC 58: TOO MUCH NOISE NOT ENOUGH TIME
THE JOURNAL OF THE INTERNATIONAL SOCIETY OF TYPOGRAPHIC DESIGNERS

DAVID JURY
HARRY MCINTOSH
ALAN ROBERTSON
ELYSSA SCHMID
CLIVE SCOTT
LORETTA STAPLES
CHRISTINE WERTHEIM

THE DESIGNERS REPUBLIC

Typographic
Country: UK

Cover Design:
The Designers Republic

domus

854
www.domusweb.it
Architettura/Design/Arte/Comunicazione
Architecture/Design/Art/Communication
Dicembre/December 2002
Euro 7.80 Italy only

Baseline
Country: UK

illustration: Jo Stankowski
Design: HDR visual communication

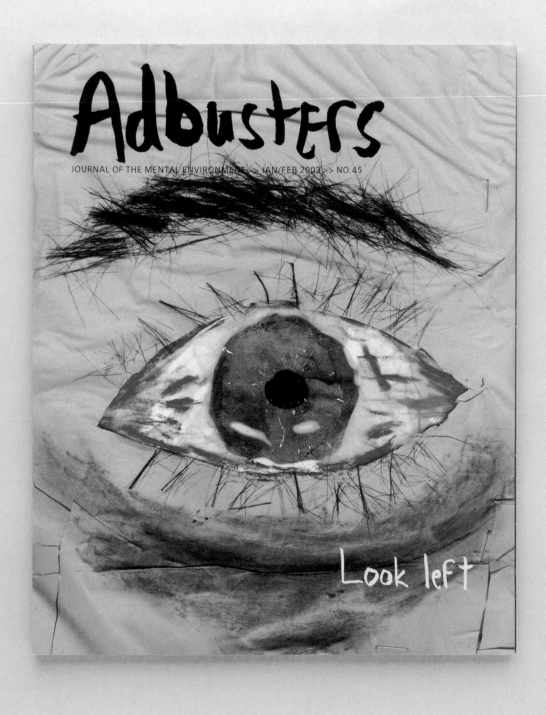

Idea
Country: Japan

Cover Design: Experimental Jetset

It is a reflex that springs from the survival instinct: protecting your own "reality" seems to be crucial for survival. The "norm" holds our values to be stable and a cult

IdN Special 02: Cultvision
Mark Magidson, Roman Coppola, Fruit Chan, Kinji Fukasaku, Jean-Pierre Jeunet, Spike Jonze, David Lynch, Lou Ye, Shinya Tsukamoto......plus CD-Rom included.

IdN
Country: Hong Kong

Creative Direction: SK Lam

Dot Dot Dot
Country: Uk/Netherlands

Cover Design: Dot Dot Dot

IdN
Country: Hong Kong

Cover Design: still from
'The Mission' by Johnnie To

I.D.

The International Design Magazine

$30 US / $42 CAN JULY/AUGUST 2003

BORDERS

2003 ANNUAL DESIGN REVIEW

consumer products
equipment
graphics
environments
furniture
packaging
concepts

7 25274 01511 5   08>

Industrial Design (later I.D.)
Country: USA

Design: unidentified

Q *Grafik* (2003–11, UK) has made the transition from print to online –
what have you gained, and what, if anything, have you lost?

A Gained: daily deadlines, access to a much larger audience. Lost: the design
element, and subsequently the visual playfulness. I'm drawn to design
magazines that are design objects in themselves, where the design of each
issue reflects the content. It's the one magazine audience that will appreciate
the design as much as the content, so it seems a missed opportunity otherwise.
The monthly magazine is the perfect playground for trying things out (with
the design and the editorial). If it doesn't work you can just try something
else next month. As an editorial team, we worked really closely with our
designers (on *Grafik*), and we always encouraged a sense of playfulness within
the design (which also reflected the attitude of the editorial). Sometimes the
balance tipped too far over to the design side, but I don't think it was ever
boring. Creating a blog post is basically like creating a list. The only day-to-day
design decisions are when to insert the images between the blocks of text,
and making the occasional animated gif. We often post pieces from the *Grafik*
archive online, and the difference is really apparent.

Q When you were the editor of a printed magazine – what were your primary
considerations for a successful cover?

A I think the magazine cover has a lot in common with a poster – it needs to
be instantly recognisable, tell you what's in the magazine, and (on a crowded
newsstand) seduce you into picking it up – all in a matter of seconds. I think
quite a different skill is required to design a cover than to create layouts, and
not everyone is good at both. One is about creating instant impact, the other
is about being much more subtle. The cover of *Grafik* was pretty much always
left until the last minute and was the cause of a fair amount of existential crises
for some of our designers. In theory, it should be a designer's dream – there
were very few commercial constraints and none of the endless straplines that
blight so many consumer mags, meaning that the cover was pretty much
a blank canvas. I think the lack of restrictions might actually have been the
cause of much of the stress.

Some of our designers tried to deal with this by creating an ongoing
series of covers, but while these looked great all together they seemed to
confuse people who bought the magazine from shops as they looked too
similar (obviously not a consideration with subscribers). We played around
with various things like wrapping the cover (suicide on the newsstand),
screenprinting it (so that every cover was different) and using various processes
such as foil blocking, UV inks and different stocks, which always drew
a very positive response.

Q Who – if anyone – is succeeding in marrying a printed design journal with
an online presence in the design world?

A I think it's really difficult. To do either well, you have to do one or the other.
If you're trying to do both, as an editor you're continually having to make
the decision whether to put a story online or 'save' it for the magazine. If
a story is featured widely online, or even just on social media, then by the
time the magazine comes out (given that most design mags are monthly or
even bimonthly/quarterly) it will be seen by readers as 'old news', even if
it is covered in much more depth within the magazine. It's hard to persuade
people to pay a premium cover price if they think they've seen the content
before, and that's why the emphasis needs to be on creating a special, collectible
object in itself. Maybe if you had two separate editorial teams and two
separate budgets it would work, but given how hard it is to monetise websites
without huge readerships, this would be pretty unlikely.

*Caroline Roberts is a journalist and author, and is currently Editor-in-Chief
of* Grafik *magazine.*

**Grafik
2003–11
UK**

Grafik 99   September 2003

Journal of the best in international
graphic design

grafik.

2003年9月1日発行・第51巻・第5号・通巻300号
毎月1日発行 ISSN 0019-1299

IDEA 300
INTERNATIONAL GRAPHIC ART

世界のデザイン誌
誠文堂新光社

アイデア

'03-09

300
50th anniversary
special issue
idea scrapbook

Dot Dot Dot
Country: UK/Netherlands

Cover Design: Dot Dot Dot

Domus
Country: Italy

Creative Director: Simon Esterson

Domus
Country: Italy

Creative Director: Simon Esterson

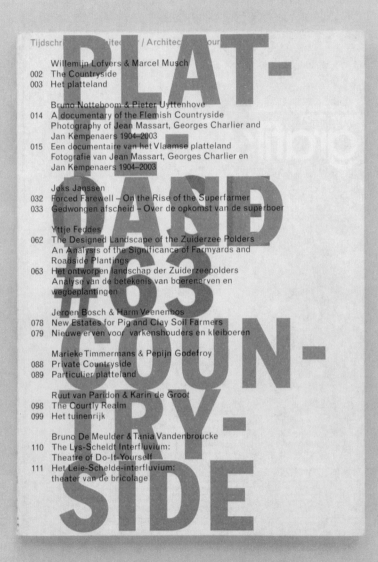

PLAT-
TELAND
#63
COUN-
TRY-
SIDE

OASE Journal for Architecture
Country: Netherlands

Cover Design:
Karel Martens, Aagje Martens,
Werkplaats Typografie

DOT DOT DOT 7
... uptight, optipessimistic art
& design magazine ... pushing
for a resolution ... in bleak
midwinter ... with local and
general aesthetics ... wound
on an ever tightening coil¹...

DOT DOT DOT 7
... uptight, optipessimistic art & design magazine ... pushing for a resolution ... in bleak midwinter ... with local and general aesthetics ... wound on an ever tightening coil⁷ ...

Dot Dot Dot
Country: UK/Netherlands

Cover Design: Dot Dot Dot

Tijdschrift voor architectuur / Architectural Journal / Zomer Summer 2004

O A S E # 6 4

ISBN 90-5662-390-7

9 789056 623906

OASE#64   NAi Uitgevers / Publishers Rotterdam

OASE Journal for Architecture
Country: Netherlands

Cover Design:
Karel Martens, Radim Pesko,
Werkplaats Typografie

215

On the magazine cover:

eye

THE INTERNATIONAL REVIEW OF GRAPHIC DESIGN · VOL.14 AUTUMN 2004

WWW.EYEMAGAZINE.COM

Eye
Country: UK

Eye logo concept: Nick Bell
Drawn: Magnus Rakeng
Art Direction: Nick Bell

Dot Dot Dot
Country: UK/Netherlands   Cover Design: Dot Dot Dot

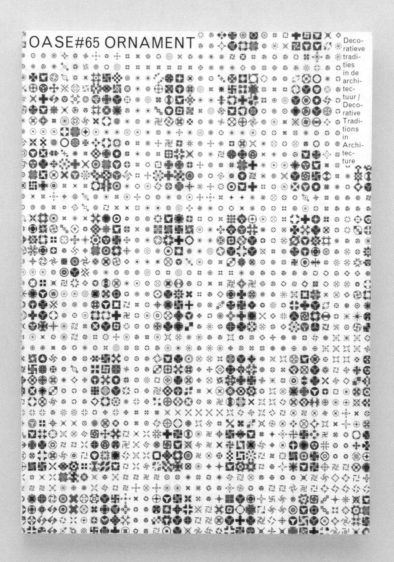

OASE#65 ORNAMENT Decoratieve tradities in de architectuur / Decorative Traditions in Architecture

OASE Journal for Architecture
Country: Netherlands

Cover Design:
Karel Martens, Aagje Martens,
Werkplaats Typografie

Idea
Country: Japan

Cover image: Mevis & Van Deursen

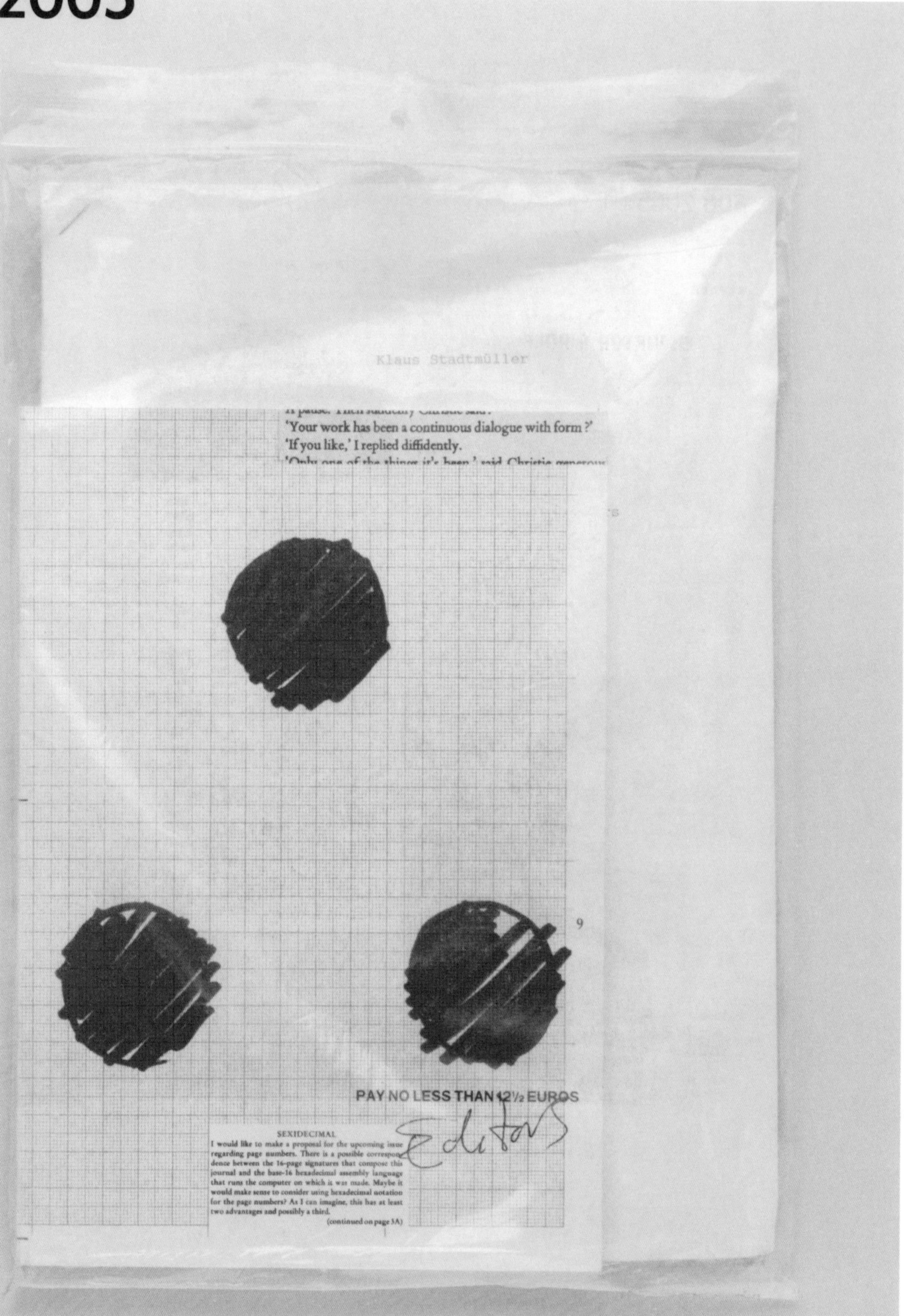

Dot Dot Dot
Country: UK/Netherlands

Cover Design: Dot Dot Dot

Design+Design

72

Euro 5,-/SFR 10,-
C 25536

Unabhängige Zeitschrift   Independent Magazine
für Design Sammler   For Design Collectors

Erscheinungszeit
Juni - Sept. 2005

Das 'hellerleuchtete objekt inmitten der
mit fontänen und guirlanden geschmückten
stände der konkurrenz'... Hans Gugelot

AJ (Architects' Journal)
Country: UK

Design: A Practice for Everyday Life
Art Editor: Sarah Douglas

Interview:
A Practice For Everyday Life

Q   Your redesign for *Architects' Journal* (1895–present, UK) received widespread coverage and praise when it was launched in 2005. Can you describe your working relationship with the editor and art editor?

A   We worked very closely with the editor Isabel Allen, the art director Sarah Douglas, and the publisher Jonathan Stock. We could take quite brave steps with their support, because they understood the implications on a practical level. In that way, they were instrumental in making some of the big changes that we proposed possible. One of the most immediately visible changes we made was to switch the large format of the magazine to a more economical journal size of 265 × 210mm.

We worked closely with the publisher to go through the production costs, and also reduced the grammage of the paper we used, in order to make a cost saving that we could put towards a commissioning budget for photography. In particular, we wanted to use this for the weekly building study, which made up a large part of each issue. Previously, the editorial team had been reliant on architects submitting their own photography, whereas commissioning their own gave them control over the art direction of each shoot, and made the aesthetic voice of the *AJ* more consistent. This was the single biggest change that gave the magazine a new, fresh look, but it was a big undertaking—anyone who has ever worked on a weekly trade magazine will understand what it took to do this. The editorial team were up for this challenge, and they went on to produce a beautiful magazine every week, so we were very pleased we pushed for this approach. This budget saving also bought us some white space to work with in the design of the inside pages.

We were also interested in how the *AJ* had become a collectable resource for subscribers and were keen to grow this as well as help find new audiences. With the new commissioned photography, there was much stronger material to work with for the covers, so we suggested removing all the taglines and pull quotes which confused and cheapened the message, and simply use strong, iconic, newsworthy building photographs, together with the date and the building and practice name of the focus study of that particular week. Another major change we made was consistency in the architectural drawings featured in the magazine. Of course, architects have their own styles in respect of this, and we felt it was very important in most cases to leave the sketches and plans as the architect provided. However, in certain cases this made the magazine quite editorially confusing and aesthetically muddled. We realised that some of the more basic plans and drawings could be re-drawn and captioned by the *AJ* art department from a set of styles that we created, which again gave much consistency to the look of the magazine.

Q   Did you feel a sense of liberation – or restraint – knowing that you were working for a design-literate audience?

A   A real sense of excitement. We love architecture, and we love magazines, so it was the perfect combination for us. We knew that by bringing in new typography and combining this with strong art direction of the photography, we were on a road to success with the magazine. The magazine team seemed to totally trust us and were happy to take risks in order to do something meaningful with the redesign. They had already gone through a long journey with the redesign, and when we were appointed they were very certain of what they wanted to achieve and had previously tested all their anxieties. We had all eyes on us as we were working on the project, as it was well known that the *AJ* was going through a redesign, but we tried not to think about that too much. Of course, there was also the unspoken factor of being a relatively young, all-female team (editor, art director and APFEL) redesigning a magazine for a historically male-dominated industry.

Q   Were you influenced by any of the great architectural magazines of the past?

A   We spent a great deal of time in the publisher EMAP's archive, looking back at previous issues of the *Architects' Journal*, *The Architectural Review* (1896–present, UK) and *Building Design* (1970–2014, UK) – there were beautiful mid-century examples of *AJ* designed by some of our heroes, and even going

AJ
1895–present
UK

AR
1896–present
UK

223

back to the magazine's origins in the early 1900s showed some incredible examples of British typography at its best. One of our favourites, the cover of *The Architectural Review* (March 1952), featured wallpaper that Eduardo Paolozzi designed for Jane Drew; the magazine later featured a Hammer Prints design, Coalface, on the cover of their October issue that year.

Looking back through the publisher's archive, the big difference we noticed within their collection was in the quality of the trade advertisements. It wasn't so much who the advertisers were, but the quality of design of the adverts themselves that have such an influence on the overall design of the magazine, as they take up a vast amount of space. Historically, trade adverts were much more beautifully designed, mainly because they were limited by the technology of letterpress, but also because they were more likely to have been laid out by a designer. In contrast, more recent issues of *AJ* had terrible trade adverts – it is a really obvious example of the consequences of the rise of desktop publishing, where anyone can design their own adverts, and the editorial designer's hands are tied because the advertiser has paid for their spot.

Other magazines we looked to were from our own collection of *Architectural Design* (1930–present, USA), issues from the 1950s to the 1970s, and a large collection of the design magazine Typographica (1949–67, UK) from the 1950s, including issue 1, published by Lund Humphries.

Q Which titles amongst the current crop of design magazines do you admire?
A It's really sad that EMAP decided, in 2014, to end the print edition of their other weekly title Building Design. It's yet another sign of the shift in magazine publishing in more general terms, as a lot of design magazines have closed down or gone online only in the last few years, and it looked for a while as if the market for printed design magazines was dwindling. We can definitely see how hard is, especially for news-focused weeklies, to keep up with the pace and immediacy of the web. But we are big believers in magazines, and in print, and it does feel like there's something lost with the closure of these print editions that their online counterparts can't quite replace. The sheer hard work from an editorial team that is involved in bringing a magazine to life, week after week, shows in the quality of the end result, but it changes readers' perceptions or expectations of the content, too. Some publishers are taking note of this, and new titles are launching that make the most of the unique qualities of print and the physicality of paper and format, in order to justify their existence. People are realising that nowadays a new magazine needs to feel precious rather than disposable, so the market looks like it's shifting permanently towards a broader range of more boutique titles rather than a short list of big, frequent, leading publications. The Internet fulfils the need for a venue for fast-paced news, shorter articles and the ability to respond and report on things as they happen, but we hope there will still always be a place for printed publications like *AJ*.

Co-founded by Kirsty Carter and Emma Thomas in 2003, APFEL works across art direction, identities, publications and exhibitions for clients from the worlds of art, fashion and publishing.

AR
1896–present
UK

AD
1930–present
UK

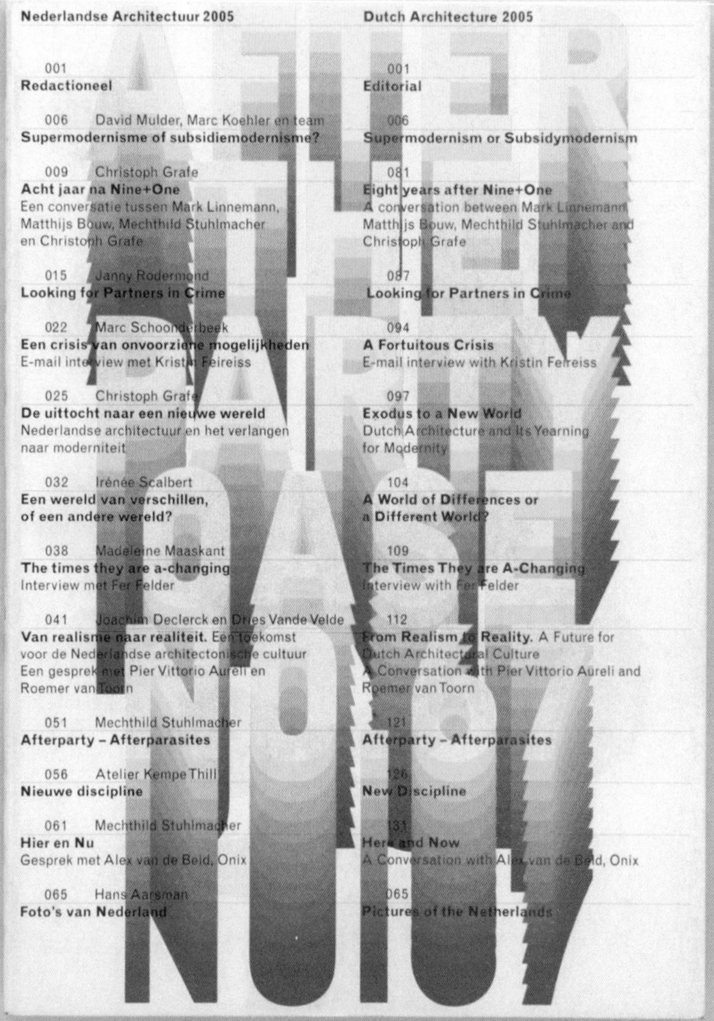

OASE Journal for Architecture
Country: Netherlands

Cover Design:
Karel Martens, Aagje Martens,
Werkplaats Typografie

Dot Dot Dot
Country: UK/Netherlands

Cover Design: Dot Dot Dot

Cover Design: Karel Martens,
Jeff Ramsey, Werkplaats Typografie

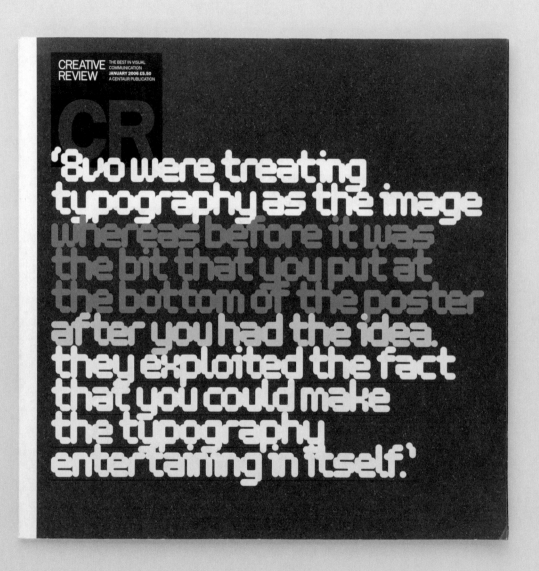

Creative Review
Country: UK

Art Director: Nathan Gale

16.03.06
ALEC FRENCH
ARCHITECTS/
SS GREAT BRITAIN

AJ

ISSN 0003-8466

£3.25

THE ARCHITECTS' JOURNAL WWW.AJPLUS.CO.UK

Circular
Country: UK

Cover Design: Lippa Pearce

Dot Dot Dot
Country: UK/Netherlands   Cover Design: Dot Dot Dot

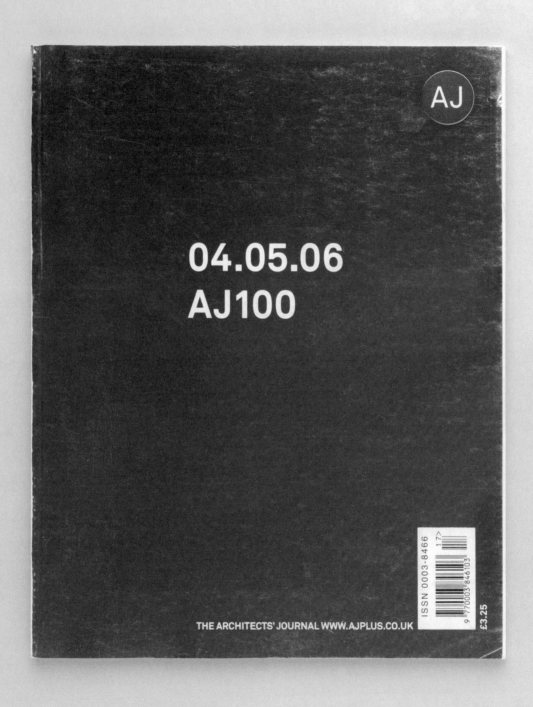

04.05.06
AJ100

THE ARCHITECTS' JOURNAL WWW.AJPLUS.CO.UK

ISSN 0003-8466

£3.25

AJ (Architects' Journal)
Country: UK

Design: A Practice for Everyday Life
Art Editor: Sarah Douglas

25.05.06
CONTAINER
ARCHITECTURE

AJ

THE ARCHITECTS' JOURNAL WWW.AJPLUS.CO.UK

ISSN 0003-8466

£3.25

AJ (Architects' Journal)
Country: UK

Design: A Practice for Everyday Life
Art Editor: Sarah Douglas

01.06.06
LE CORBUSIER/
STUTTGART

AJ

THE ARCHITECTS' JOURNAL WWW.AJPLUS.CO.UK

ISSN 0003-8466

£3.25

OASE Journal for Architecture
Country: Netherlands

Cover Design:
Karel Martens, Layla Tweedie-Cullen,
Werkplaats Typografie

Creative Review
Country: UK

Art Director: Nathan Gale

Grafik
Country: UK

Cover Design: Nick Tweedie

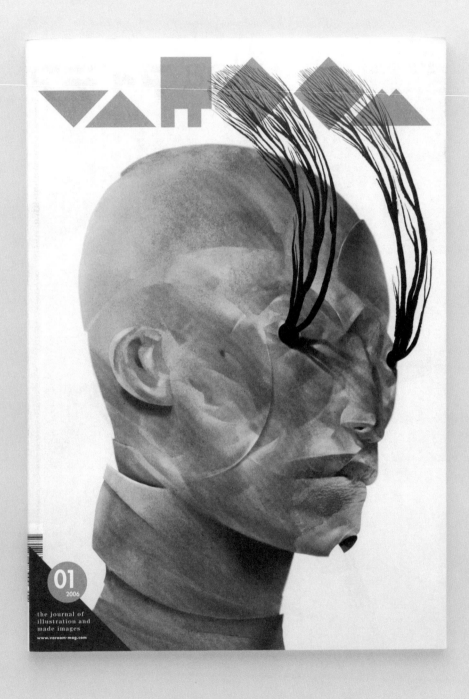

Varoom
Country: UK

Cover image: Sam Weber
Cover design: Non Format

Idea
Country: Japan

Cover Design: Edward Fella

Tijdschrift voor architectuur / Journal for Architecture

Stedelijke
formatie &
collectieve
ruimten

Urban
Formation &
Collective
Spaces

OASE 71

OASE Journal for Architecture
Country: Netherlands

Cover Design:
Karel Martens, Aagje Martens,
Werkplaats Typografie

December/January
2006/07 £8

Grafik
Country: UK

Cover Design: SEA

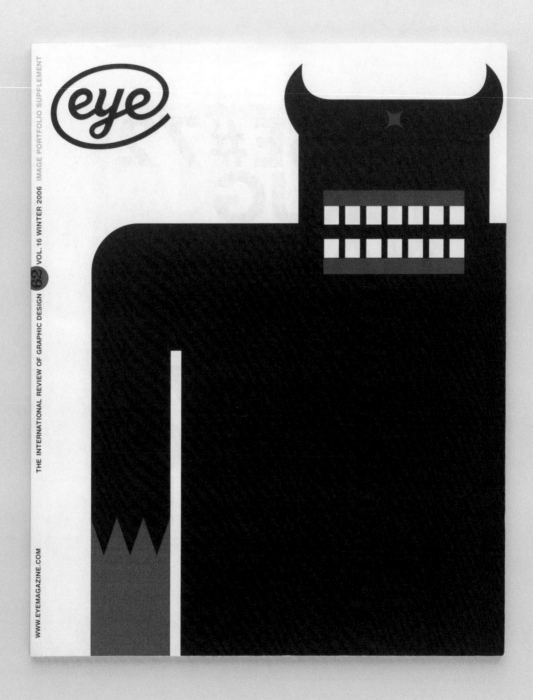

'Punto Zero, 2003,' :
Motomichi Nakamura
Art Direction: Simon Esterson

Eye
Country: UK

OASE#72
TERUG
NAAR
SCHOOL

Tijdschrift voor architectuur Journal for Architecture   NAi Uitgevers/ Publishers Rotterdam

OASE#72
BACK TO
SCHOOL

OASE Journal for Architecture
Country: Netherlands

Cover Design:
Karel Martens, Guillaume Mojon,
Werkplaats Typografie

issue 01 . volume 01
MARCH 2007

MONOCLE

A BRIEFING ON GLOBAL AFFAIRS, BUSINESS, CULTURE & DESIGN

Japan Takes Aim

Asia's most advanced fleet looks beyond the horizon
MONOCLE gains exclusive access to the world's only non-existent navy, *page 033*

Ⓐ AFFAIRS
China in Africa
Questioning Chile's Finance Minister

Ⓑ BUSINESS
Ensanada: the about to boom town
Germany's happiest wine exporter

Ⓒ CULTURE
On air in Afghanistan
India's new daily

Ⓓ DESIGN
Brazil's first family of hospitality
Beauty school in Taipei

Ⓔ EDITS
Our inventory of all you need in life
Plus: Move to Genoa and NBC's
Ann Curry on her last order

EXPO
A portrait of Europe's highest city.
+ Kitakoga, the Monocle manga

Creative Director:
Richard Spencer Powell
Art Director: Ken Leung

TM (Typographische Monatsblätter)   Design: Lukas Hartmann
Country: Switzerland   Courtesy of syndicom

gra fik fig fik one zero fl five f zero

Special Report
Process
Profile
Fuel

April 2007 £8

Grafik
Country: UK

Cover Design: SEA

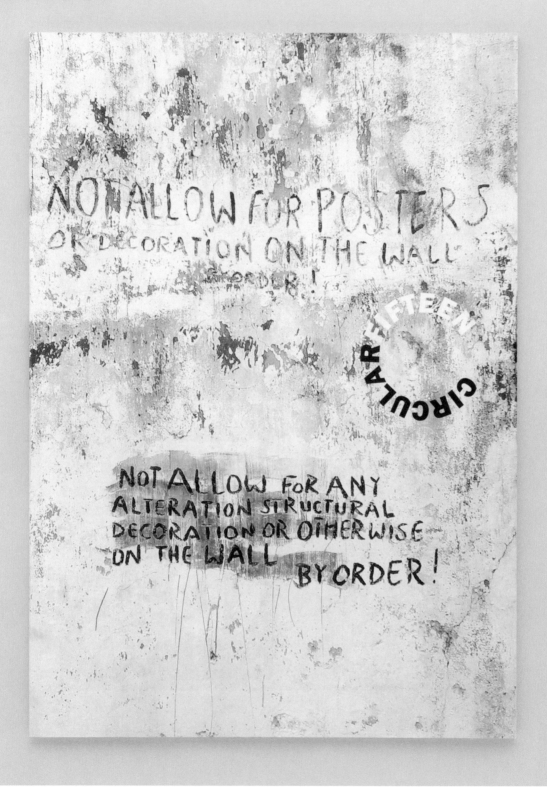

Circular
Country: UK

Cover Design: Domenic Lippa,
Jeremy Kunze, Pentagram

Grafik
Country: UK

Cover Design: SEA

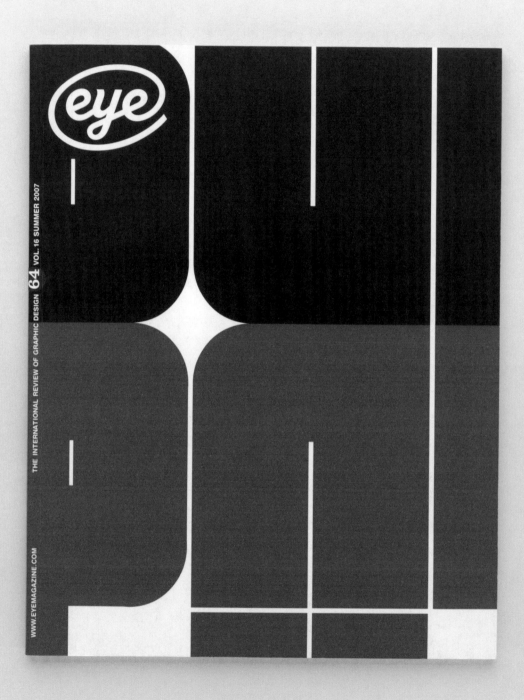

eye

THE INTERNATIONAL REVIEW OF GRAPHIC DESIGN 64 VOL. 16 SUMMER 2007

WWW.EYEMAGAZINE.COM

Eye
Country: UK

Detail from poster: Theo Ballmer
Art Director: Simon Esterson

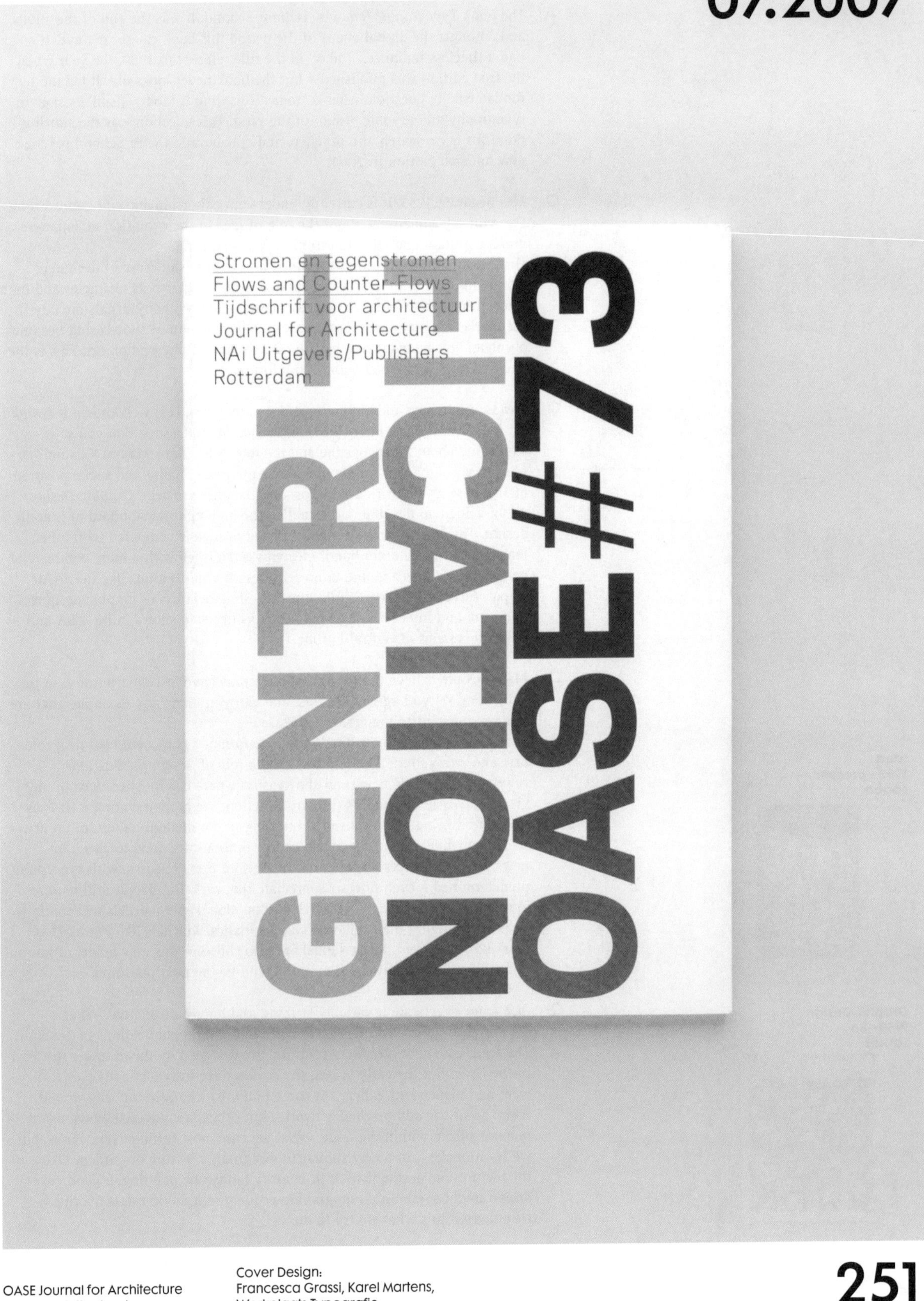

Stromen en tegenstromen
Flows and Counter-Flows
Tijdschrift voor architectuur
Journal for Architecture
NAi Uitgevers/Publishers
Rotterdam

GENTRIFICATION OASE #73

Cover Design:
Francesca Grassi, Karel Martens,
Werkplaats Typografie

Q What was the first design publication that caught your attention – and why?

A The book *Typography Today* by Helmut Schmid. It was the end of the 1990s, and amongst the digital chaos of the period this book caught my eye. It had a timeless radiance. 'Today' in the title referred to 1980, the year when the first edition was published – but the book never looks old. It led me to fundamentally question 'what is "today"' or 'what is Modern(ism)' in modern typography and graphic design in the West. This question was the starting point for my research and practice, and collaboration with Schmid for the new updated edition in 2003.

Q *Idea* began in 1953. It is currently under your editorship and still going strong. Can you say something about the role of *Idea* in the evolution of Japanese graphic design, and why you think it is so enduring?

A Historically, the magazine functioned as a unique showcase of designers worldwide, rather than as a critical platform. Thanks to its character and high price, it has survived and avoided competing with other journals directly in the market. After the rise of the Internet, its function of showcasing became obsolete, but the magazine has found its role as a physical object. This is the story so far. I am not sure about the future.

Q *Idea* is well known and highly respected in the West. Less well known is *Graphic Design* – which came later (1959) and lasted for 100 issues. Can you say something about this magazine and the role of its editor Masaru Katsumi?

A Masaru was an agent for change, developing the quality and social position of Japanese graphic design. In post-war Japanese society, *Graphic Design* was a vehicle to develop and establish the high cultural standard of graphic design. The content was very curated and academic compared with other magazines. On the other hand, *Idea* was established with a more commercial perspective. It was a venue to present design organisations like the JAAC (Japan Advertising Artist Club), the largest association of graphic designers in Japan, and international events such as like solo shows in the USA and poster biennales in central Europe.

Q Many people believe that design publications have lost their purpose in the online era. Do you agree with this, and can you name any examples that are proving relevant to the modern era?

A That opinion has some truth. Any media format has its own historical role, task and motivation. As I said before, the role of design publications in introducing trade news and showcasing works has finished. *Idea* (in my view) has already ended its primary function. We are renovating it. It is as if we are turning an old business building into a modern gallery or library.

Meanwhile, design blogs and online journals are good to check for news. But the sources are often no more than press releases, with everything predetermined – even how to appreciate the work. But people still require journals with deep insight, research and opinion. Paper journals will continue to exist, changing their role and characteristics. Journals like *Works That Work* (2013–present, Netherlands) are also showing this new model of journal publishing. Radio shows and movies could be the next platforms.

Q *Idea* front covers are invariably striking and highly distinctive. What is the secret of good cover design for *Idea* and design publications in general?

A The front covers of *Idea* were traditionally designed by the designer featured in the issue. For the early issues, the covers were truly distinctive, as if they were an independent gallery. At some point, we changed the way we did them. Some are still original artworks, but others are directed by us, using materials from within the issue. What we care most for in covers varies, but we try to make it in a way similar to designing a picture or garden. Like the picturesque aesthetic of 18th-century landscape painting, a good cover design might summon a typographic-esque or a graphic-esque quality. Or at least that's what we try to do.

Kiyonori Muroga has been Editor-in-Chief of Tokyo-based Idea *since 2002. He writes on graphic design and typography, and lectures at schools and universities across Japan.*

Idea
1953—present
Japan

Graphic Design
1959—86
Japan

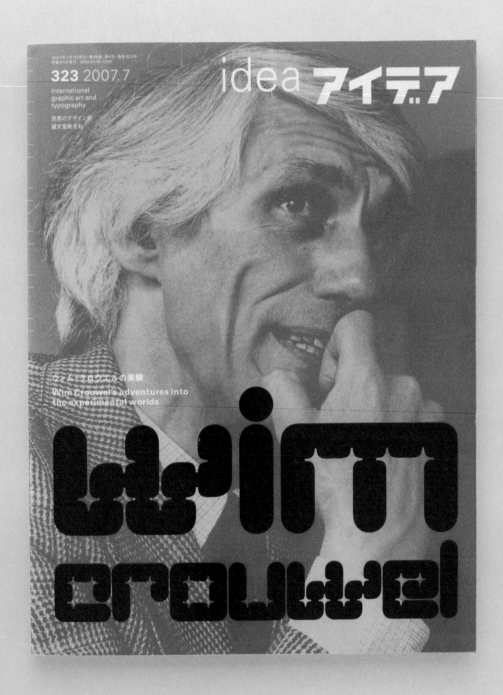

Idea
Country: Japan

Cover Design: Shirai Design Studio

Varoom
Country: UK

Cover image: Bela Borsodi
Cover Design: Non-Format

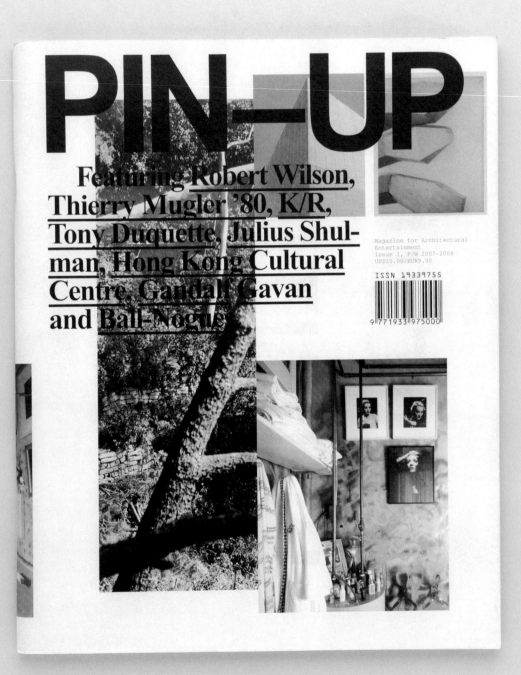

PIN-UP

Featuring Robert Wilson, Thierry Mugler '80, K/R, Tony Duquette, Julius Shulman, Hong Kong Cultural Centre, Gandalf Gavan and Ball-Nogues

Magazine for Architectural Entertainment
Issue 3, F/W 2007-2008
US$10.00/EUR9.90

ISSN 19339755

9 771933 975000

Cover Design:
Dylan Fracareta, Geoffrey Han

OASE Journal for Architecture
Country: Netherlands

Cover Design: Karel Martens,
Enrico Bravi, Werkplaats Typografie

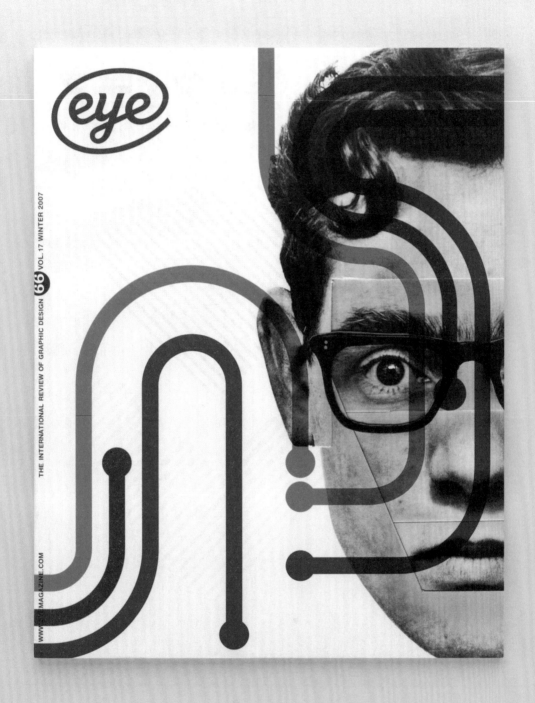

Eye
Country: UK

Detail from Photofit:
Ken Garland & Assoc.
Art Director: Simon Esterson

Idea
Country: Japan

Cover Design: Kazunari Hattori

Dot Dot Dot
Country: UK/Netherlands   Cover Design: Dot Dot Dot

Creative Review
Country: UK

Art Director: Paul Pensom

PIN—UP

Featuring
Annabelle Selldorf,
Christian Lacroix,
Madelon Vriesendorp,
Roger Bundschuh,
Florian Slotawa,
Lustron, Hotel Estela,
EXYZT, Brussels,
and Aranda/Lasch.

Magazine for Architectural
Entertainment
Issue 4, Summer, 2008
US$10.00/EUR9.90

ISSN 19339755

9 771933 975000

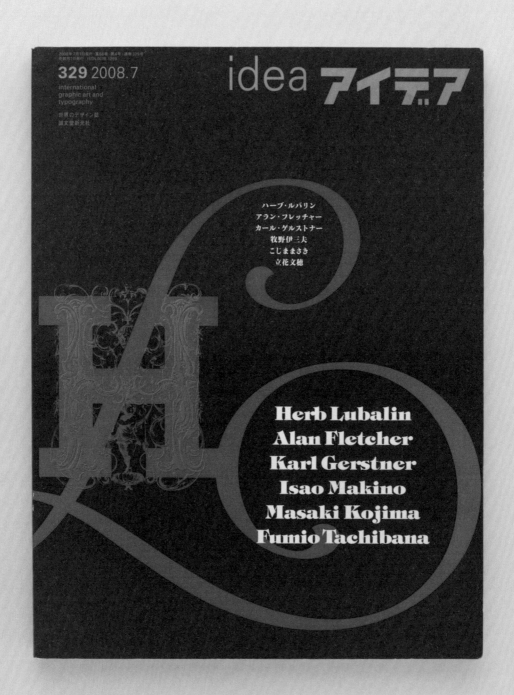

Idea
Country: Japan

Cover Design: Shirai Design Studio

IT'S WHAT YOUR RIGHT ARM'S FOR
WE DO IT YOUR WAY
HEAD FOR THE BORDER
WE KEEP YOUR PROMISES
ONE LEG AT A TIME
WE'RE NUMBER TWO. WE TRY HARDER
WOT A LOT I GOT
FINGER-LICKIN' GOOD
WHILE IN EUROPE, PICK UP AN UGLY EUROPEAN
A LITTLE DAB'LL DO YA
CLEANS ROUND THE BEND
GEE, I WISH I HAD A NICKEL
JUST IMAGINE
LIVE TODAY. TOMORROW WILL COST MORE
ONLY 1 OUT OF 25 MEN IS COLOR BLIND. THE OTHER 24 JUST DRESS THAT WAY
STOPS HALITOSIS!
MAKE YOURSELF HEARD
TASTE AS GOOD AS IT SMELLS
WE SELL MORE CARS THAN FORD, CHRYSLER, CHEVROLET, AND BUICK COMBINED
LIMITED EDITION OF UNLIMITED IDEAS
PURE GENIUS
IT IS. ARE YOU?
SOFT, STRONG AND VERY LONG
PREPARE TO WANT ONE
IT'S SO BIG, YOU'VE GOTTA GRIN TO GET IT IN
THINK DIFFERENT
HELLO BOYS
BLOW SOME MY WAY
THE GENUINE ARTICLE
COME TO WHERE THE FLAVOR IS

FUTU
Country: Poland
Cover Design: Matt Willey

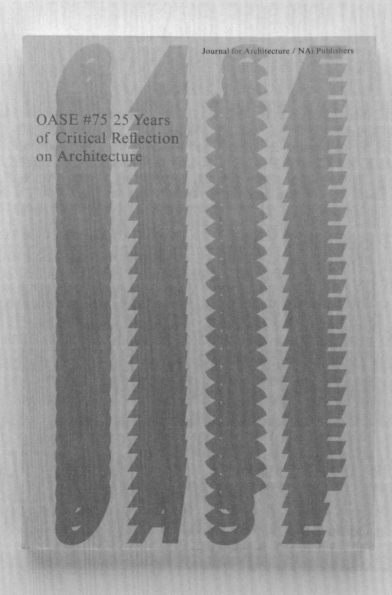

OASE #75 25 Years
of Critical Reflection
on Architecture

Journal for Architecture / NAi Publishers

OASE Journal for Architecture
Country: Netherlands

Cover Design:
Joris Kritis, Karel Martens,
Werkplaats Typografie

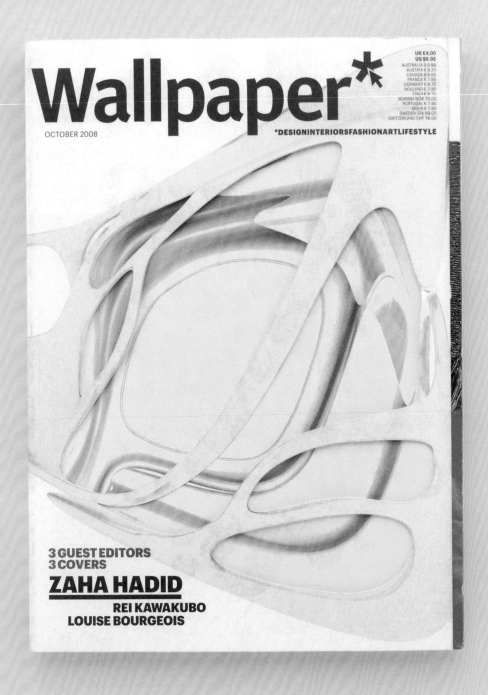

Wallpaper*

OCTOBER 2008

*DESIGNINTERIORSFASHIONARTLIFESTYLE

UK £4.00
US $8.95
AUSTRALIA $ 9.99
AUSTRIA € 9.35
CANADA $ 8.95
FRANCE € 7.90
GERMANY € 9.75
HOLLAND € 7.90
ITALY € 8.70
NORWAY NOK 79.00
PORTUGAL € 7.90
SPAIN € 7.90
SWEDEN SEK 69.00
SWITZERLAND CHF 16.00

3 GUEST EDITORS
3 COVERS
ZAHA HADID
REI KAWAKUBO
LOUISE BOURGEOIS

illustrated lettering edition.

09
2009

Varoom
Country: UK

Cover image: Alex Trochut
Cover design: Non Format

DOT DOT DOT 17 (read) (spoken) (delivered)
from two (lecterns) (supports) (props) at
the Embankment Galleries, Somerset House,
London on 29/30/31 October 2008 in advance
of being (transcribed) (translated) (transfixed)
and returned at the close of the exhibition
(multiplied) (published) (distributed) on
21 December 2008.

Graphic
Country: South Korea

Cover Design: Na Kim

The International Review of Graphic Design

73 AUTUMN 2009

PHOTOGRAPHY SPECIAL

'Napkin': Hendrik Kerstens
Art Director: Simon Esterson

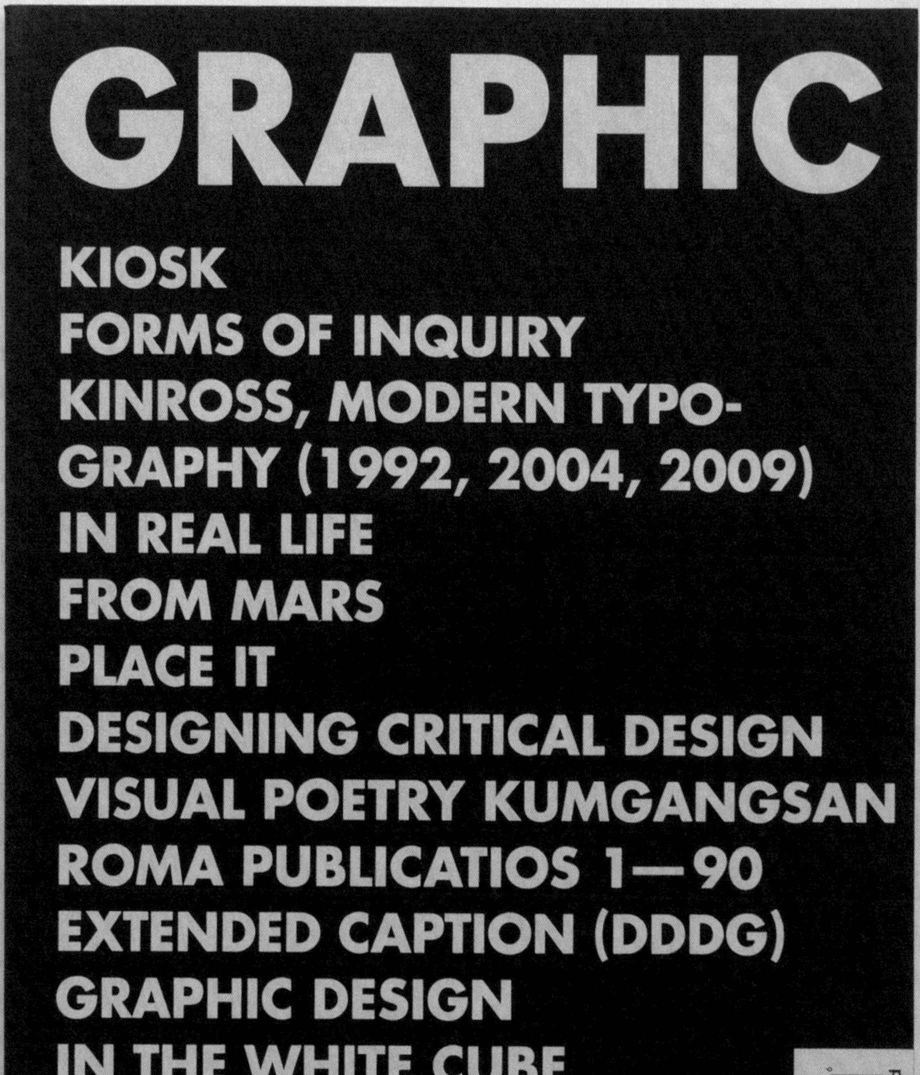

GRAPHIC

KIOSK
FORMS OF INQUIRY
KINROSS, MODERN TYPO-
GRAPHY (1992, 2004, 2009)
IN REAL LIFE
FROM MARS
PLACE IT
DESIGNING CRITICAL DESIGN
VISUAL POETRY KUMGANGSAN
ROMA PUBLICATIOS 1—90
EXTENDED CAPTION (DDDG)
GRAPHIC DESIGN
IN THE WHITE CUBE
ON PURPOSE

QUARTERLY GRAPHIC MAGAZINE #11 AUTUMN 2009 IDEAS OF DESIGN EXHIBITION 디자인 전시의 개념들

propaganda
ISSN 1975-7905
값 15,000원

Graphic
Country: South Korea

Cover Design: Na Kim

Dot Dot Dot
Country: UK/Netherlands

Cover Design: Dot Dot Dot

CREATIVE REVIEW
The Best in Visual Communication
A Centaur Publication. October 2009. £5.70

CR

Creative Review
Country: UK

Art Director: Paul Pensom

GRAPHIC

propaganda

定 15,000원

9 771975 790500 94

ISSN 1975–7905

QUARTERLY GRAPHIC MAGAZINE
#12 WINTER 2009
MANYSTUFF SPECIAL ISSUE
계간그래픽매거진 매니스터프 스페셜 이슈

Idea
Country: Japan

Cover Design: Shirai Design Studio

BACK COVER

DESIGN GRAPHIQUE, TYPOGRAPHIE, ETC.
GRAPHIC DESIGN, TYPOGRAPHY, ETC.

Åbäke | Alexandre Dimos | Anthony Froshaug | Aurélien Froment |
Richard Hollis | Jean-Yves Jouannais | Robin Kinross | Metahaven |
Didier Semin | Yann Sérandour | Benjamin Thorel | Raphaël Zarka |

HIVER/PRINTEMPS 2010
WINTER/SPRING 2010

3

Back Cover
Country: France

Cover Design: deValence

Process Journal
Country: Australia

Art Direction & Design:
Thomas Williams, Nicholas Cary

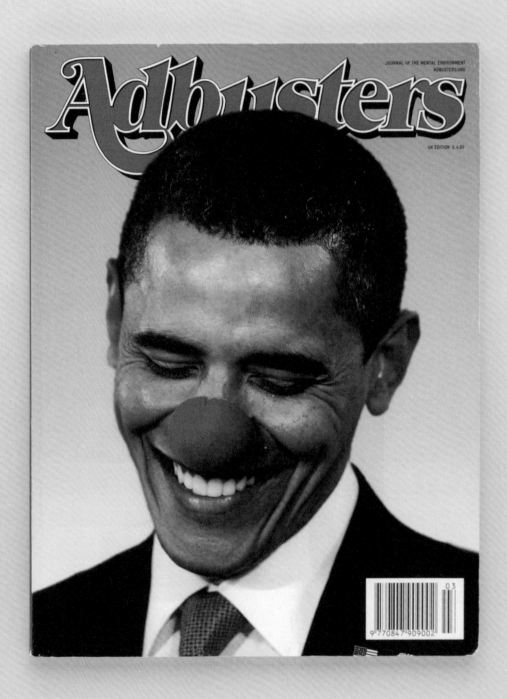

Adbusters
Country: Canada
Design: unidentified

Adbusters
Country: Canada

Guest Art Director: Pedro Inoue

KYOORIUS 8 MAGAZINE
Branding, Advertising, Design and Visual Communications

Kyoorius
Country: India

Creative Director: Kay H Khoo

Process Journal
Edition Four

Browns
Christopher Doyle
Toko
Give Up Art
Nice Device
KentLyons
Schwartzco
Build
Design Project
Tonatiuh Ambrosetti
Inhouse Design
Tom Munckton
Marque

First Quarter 2011   ISSN
Aud $25.00 Inc. GST   1837-7807

Process Journal
Country: Australia

Art Direction & Design:
Nicholas Cary, Thomas Williams

Circular Seventeen

A publication of the Typographic Circle

It's been a great year for our talks and we've seen a lot of great work—Airside, Paul Davis, Michael Wolff, Studio 8, Pentagram and Research Studios, to name just a few. In light of this, we decided to make their work the real hero in this issue of Circular.

I hope you enjoy the chance to further ponder/drool over what you saw, and, if you didn't make it on the evening, a tasty taster of what you missed.

I think it's clear now that the Typographic Circle isn't just about kerning, counters or Cooper Black, but also a celebration of the fantastic and varied typographic work that is out there.

Our website is proving to be invaluable, so please do keep in touch and send us your thoughts. Your support at the events, and as members, is so important to making it all happen.

Alongside our usual programme of speakers, we are hoping that this year will be an excellent opportunity for a retrospective exhibition, in recognition of the Circle's existence since 1976. We'll keep you posted.

As you know, the committee are all volunteers, so a big thank you from me to all of them, and to Domenic Lippa and his team for another beautifully designed Circular.

Very much hope to see you at our future events as often as you can make it.

John Bateson
Chairman

Aa/SW/HK

One Work
Art directed and designed by Aa/SW/HK, 'One Work' is a unique series of books published by Afterall Books, each of which presents a single work of art considered in detail by a single author. Designed to complement Afterall journal, the series features bespoke typefaces designed by Aa/SW/HK.

Ergonomics – Real Design
An exhibition identity, applied graphics, bespoke display typeface and brochure design commissioned for the 2009–2010 'Ergonomics' exhibition at the Design Museum, London.

Zadie
Inspired by Edwardian railings surrounding the Royal Army Medical College in London, and later developed as a headline face for Vogue UK, the font features on the 2009 cover of the Zadie Smith bestseller 'On Beauty'. The lettering has been developed into a full font with an accompanying solid serif in two styles.

Samuel Beckett – Complete Works
A series of book cover designs commissioned by Faber & Faber in 2009, featuring Aa/Type's industrial typeface, 'Beckett'.

5
Italian King of the B's (detail)
A film and events poster, created in 2009 for the Tate Modern, London.

6
Europa (detail)
A film and events poster, created in 2009 for the Tate Modern, London.
Typefaces commercially available at several type cuts.

Hat-trick Design

Illuminating London
An environmental project for Land Securities featuring a typeface of illuminated letters – each letter telling a different story for passers by to discover.

7
War Stamp
A special stamp, issued by the Royal Mail, to commemorate the 90th anniversary of the Battle of Passchendaele. The second in a series of three, the design extends the theme of photographs of Poppies with the centre of the Poppy incorporating images of the battlefields.

8
Royal Shakespeare Company Stamps
A set of stamps to celebrate the 50th anniversary of the Royal Shakespeare Company. The first set was in collaboration with Marion Deuchars.

9
Deck
A self-initiated project to create a typographic deck of playing cards. Produced as a set of cards and a limited edition poster in partnership with a paper and print company.

Jonathan Barnbrook

11
17th Biennale of Sydney
The graphics drew inspiration from the work of Harry Smith, experimental filmmaker, artist, record collector, bohemian and mystic – who released the hugely influential Anthology of American Folk Music in 1952. This expansive visual identity was devised to communicate the eclectic motifs located ideas that informed the concepts behind Australia's largest contemporary art festival.

12
Hopeless Diamond
Hopeless Diamond – a name derived from the somewhat derisory term test pilots gave to an early model of the F-117 due to its unusual structure is a display typeface inspired by the dimensionality of 19th century carved lettering and the radical forms of the B-2 Spirit Stealth Bomber and the F-117 Nighthawk Stealth Strike aircraft. This typeface contains three different styles, each with an italic and an alternate character set that can be used to generate a number of interesting permutations.

13
Love Music Love Food
A typographic identity for the UK charity Love Music Love Food, who work in collaboration with the Teenage Cancer Trust. The type treatment uses a customised version of the Virus font Moron as a base to create a vibrant, pop-inspired wordmark.

Fred Flade

14
1971: Helvetica (detail)
Celebrating 50 years of Helvetica, 50 designers were each given a specific area from which to pick an event and design a 50×50cm poster, only using Helvetica. Fred was given 1971 and chose the cult classic A Clockwork Orange, by Stanley Kubrick. The poster features 1,000 numbers representing each second of the film, with quotes dropped in exactly when they occur.

15
Moran Process (detail)
A design suggesting the chaotic and often random nature of the creative process to map out 12 milestones of a design project. The project, called 'Moran', was initiated by Month. The brief was to depict a poster using only one colour, responding to one specific word, in this case 'process'.

Michael Wolff

16
Bowyers
An early use of nostalgia in a national food brand. Bowyers' pie mark was a combination of photography and illustration. With large old fashioned images on modern articulated trucks, the design was a dramatic success. Bowyers inspired many companies, especially in the food business, and nostalgia became a part of modern graphic language.

17
Halfords
M&, a in the paint industry. The top three were rarely tinted in size and its survival was in doubt. However, our trade liked it because it was small, easy fighting for survival. That led to the for the Halfords and the energy.

18
Bovis
Bovis was the UK's most successful builder, on its way to becoming a major international construction company. An example of an unusual and famous mark helping to create an unusual and famous brand.

19
Pyjoni
Pyjoni is the new name for a Russian credit and savings bank. The name meant 'Let's go' in a down-to-earth, 'together' sense. The brand avoids the international logo and interpts style adopted by 'westernised' banks in Russia. Designed to appeal to ordinary people throughout the country, it has a real sense, sometimes woven into traditional Russian lore. In keeping with the bank's huge following on the way, creating a warm and welcoming atmosphere. During Russia's long cold winters, tea is served from samovars to encourage people to feel at home.

Paul Davis

20
Get The Sleeve
This is the story of a product, or brand, or thing called

Made Thought

Established & Sons
A 6×6 metre space at the exhibition at Salone Internazionale del Mobile, 2006. The brand developed for Established & Sons created an identity that transcended the individual names of the prestigious designers it employs.

22
Stella McCartney
Brand design, décor and packaging for 'Stella In Two' by Stella McCartney. A packaging solution that blurs the boundaries between a vintage-inspired aesthetic and modern sensibility.

23
Established & Sons
Stationery for a brand that reflects the values of traditional British manufacturing and cutting-edge design.

24
Design Miami 2006
Invitation pack and VIP card for Design Miami/Basel, 2006. The Design Miami event, which takes place annually in Basel and Miami, demanded a brand identity that would immediately imbue it with a sense of legitimacy and authority.

25
Design Miami 2007
Invitation, exhibition catalogue and save the date for Design Miami/Basel. The use of an iconic angled bow gives Design Miami a powerful and memorable identifier across a range of brand applications.

Anthony Burrill

26
Think About All You Say
This set of posters were the result of a combination from the British Council. The aim was to show resourceful practice of design, to create a work imagining the resources of the city of Lisbon. The research into vernacular typography was done in Lisbon and the posters were created in, of and around the city.

27
Don't Say Nothing – Say Something
A poster from an on-going series of woodblock prints made with Adams of Rye. "I like the double negative in the phrase. I like to use words in a playful and humorous way, while at the same time trying to get over a deeper message."

28
Oil & Water Do Not Mix
Made in collaboration with Happiness. Brussels who find the idea to produce a fund-raising poster appealing, proceed using oil from the Gulf of Mexico spill, with the money raised being donated to local initiatives on the Gulf coast dealing with the environmental disaster.

Manny Ling

29
26 Letters
A work inspired by the analogy that letters of the alphabet are like a big family, all playing their parts to create the harmonious whole.

Richard Morrison

31
Quadrophenia
Director: Frank Roddam
Release: 1979
"Quadrophenia was one of the very first screenprints I did. It was a little bit unconventional. I was in the right place at the right time, but then again, in the business where reputations and relationships are gold, you make your own luck."

32
Brazil
Director: Terry Gilliam
Release: 1985
"Visually limited and inspiring, Brazil is a good example of a title sequence that's very much part of a creative process between the designer and the director."

Studio 8 Design

33
CSSD Invite
An exuberant new identity for the Central School of Speech and Drama which retains a sense of heritage and prestige. From redesigning all playbills and other theatrical ephemera, Typerty's bespoke typeface, was created which references the neon-tube lighting outside its theatre signs. Working with Dalton Maag, and using the school's original sign as the base, an italic stroke was added to each character to give a family of three styles – a solid, an italic and a hairline which have then used to create the new logo. Along with a bold palette of colours, Typerty was applied to a range of branded materials, including the A2 invitation which saw them all together at the launch event to reveal the new typeface and brand colours.

34
Elephant Magazine
Issue 1
Winter 2009–2010
Cover image by Pedro Inoue

35
Elephant Magazine
Issue 2
Spring 2010
Cover image by Giles Revell

GBH

36
GL5
The identity for Philippe Starck's GL5 Hotel in Beverly Hills combines traditional heraldic styling with the subversive themes of its design to capture its flavour of offbeat decadence.

37
PUMA Eco-table
The PUMA Eco-table is a system used for the sports brand on all packaging and product to communicate

and an elegant setting conveying carnival-day credentials.

38
The City Of Light, Flos 2006
Legendary Italian lighting manufacturer Flos adds multinational lighting products to its range and launches with 'The City Of Light' devised from more than 250 individual products.

Airside

39
The Wallpaper* Letters
A and 3
Designed by Malika Favre for the Sex and Art issue of Wallpaper*, this sexy typeface features a selection of leather ladies forming some very naughty letters of the alphabet.

40
The Triptych
For his first official compilation, Fred Deakin was looking to push the boundaries and explore Airside's graphic style. The trademark abstract patterns that had characterised Lemon Jelly's previous releases were handled on a series of key placements and by experimenting with these came a sense of more angular repeat set which mirrored the eclectic flow of the music itself.

41
Stay With You CD Single

42
Spacewalk CD Single
Lemon Jelly's album and single packaging weren't because any time soft, rather the traditional jewel-case in favour of elaborately designed sleeves. Airside explored the rhetoric and abstract, generally Lemon Jelly's music suggested, and turned the act of opening each sleeve into an experience itself.

Membership
The Typographic Circle was formed in 1976 to bring together anyone with an interest in type and typography. We host a core of youth organisation run entirely by volunteers staging a wide variety of type-related events, including our regular lectures and the annual TDC exhibition. A series of highly collectable limited edition posters – mostly designed by our guest speakers – are presented to our members at each event.

Before being serious about type, we're also a very sociable organisation with a reputation for putting enjoyable events. We try hard not to over-price or be stuffy or elitist. There are so many motivations. For those who wish to join, individual membership costs just £30 per year, but voice membership is just half the student rate for an affordable £15.

If you would like to become a member, please register via our website. You can also find further information about the benefits of membership, and join our mailing list. www.typocircle.com.

Check out our Facebook, LinkedIn and Twitter groups to receive information on all upcoming talks and join in with the discussions.

archphoto 2.0

00

_plug_in

1861 — 2011

Archphoto 2.0
Country: Italy

Design: Daniele De Batté,
Davide Sossi (Artiva Design)

Archphoto 2.0
Country: Italy

Design: Daniele De Batté,
Davide Sossi (Artiva Design)

GRAPHIC

Quarterly Graphic Magazine
#19 Autumn 2011
What A Beautiful Book Is
Best Book Competitions Issue
아름다운 책이란 무엇인가
베스트 도서 컴피티션 이슈

De Best
Verzorgde
Boeken
Les plus
beaux livres
français
Die schönsten
Schweizer
Bücher
Svensk
Bokkonst

Graphic
Country: South Korea

Cover Design: Na Kim

Slanted
Country: Germany

Art Direction:
Flo Gartner, Lars Harmsen

Inventario
Country: Italy

Art Director: Artemio Croatto

étapes : design and visual culture

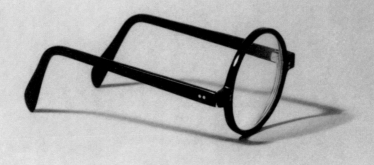

ISSUE 26
WINTER 2011
GB £25
DE €28   IT €24
ISSN 1767-4751
PRINTED IN FRANCE
PYRAMYD

Slanted
Country: Germany

Art Direction:
Flo Gartner, Lars Harmsen

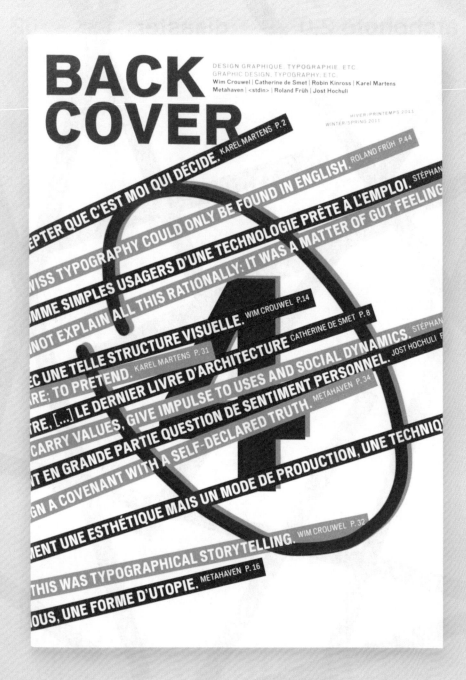

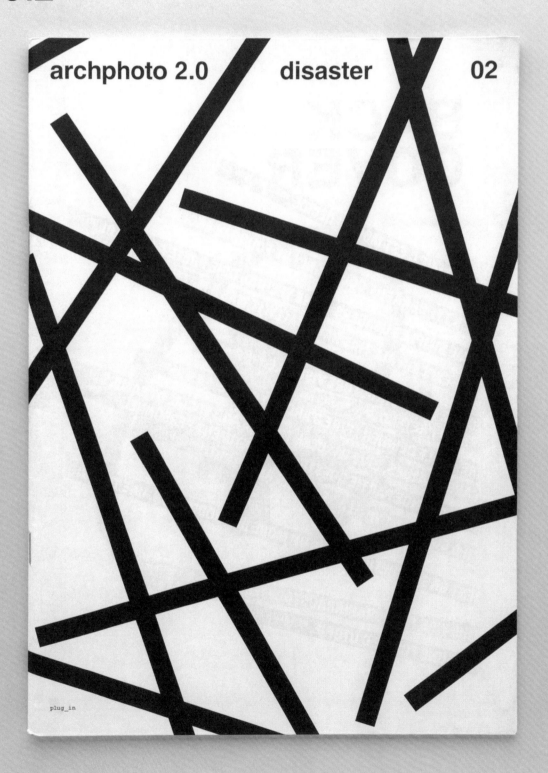

archphoto 2.0   disaster   02

plug_in

Archphoto 2.0
Country: Italy

Cover Design: Artiva Design

dni16

Paris era
una fiesta...
de diseño
**Radiografía
de la Lamy
Safari**
El clásico
secreto de Mies,
Le Corbusier
y los Eames
**Diseño
editorial:
Unit Editions**

revista de diseño
nacional e internacional
Marzo 2012

vigencia

ARQ
ClarínX

Profile
Daniel Freytag
Dowling Duncan

Feature
SEA Design
Unit Editions
Wieden+Kennedy
NB Studio
Ultra Studio
DesignStudio
Underware
BVD
Kobi Benezri Studio

Essay
Dellano Pereira
Clinton Duncan

First Quarter 2012
AUD $25.00 inc. GST
ISSN 1837-7807

Process Journal
Edition Six

Process Journal

Edition
Six

Process Journal
Country: Australia

Design: Made Publishers,
Thomas Williams, Amber Hourigan

Wallpaper*
Country: UK

Cover Illustration: Noma Bar
Art Director: Meirion Pritchard

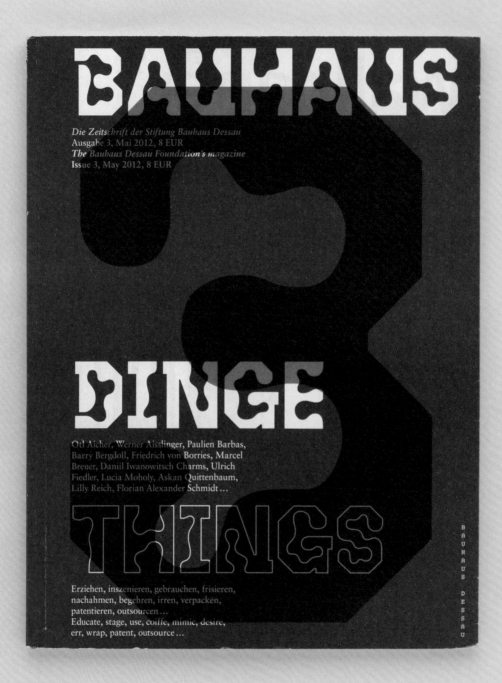

BAUHAUS

Die Zeitschrift der Stiftung Bauhaus Dessau
Ausgabe 3, Mai 2012, 8 EUR
The Bauhaus Dessau Foundation's magazine
Issue 3, May 2012, 8 EUR

DINGE

Otl Aicher, Werner Aisslinger, Paulien Barbas,
Barry Bergdoll, Friedrich von Borries, Marcel
Breuer, Daniil Iwanowitsch Charms, Ulrich
Fiedler, Lucia Moholy, Askan Quittenbaum,
Lilly Reich, Florian Alexander Schmidt ...

THINGS

Erziehen, inszenieren, gebrauchen, frisieren,
nachahmen, begehren, irren, verpacken,
patentieren, outsourcen ...
Educate, stage, use, coiffe, mimic, desire,
err, wrap, patent, outsource ...

BAUHAUS DESSAU

Bauhaus
Country: Germany

Cover Design: novamondo

Cover Design: Based on Knoll
poster by Massimo Vignelli 1966.
Art Director: Simon Esterson

06—08.2012

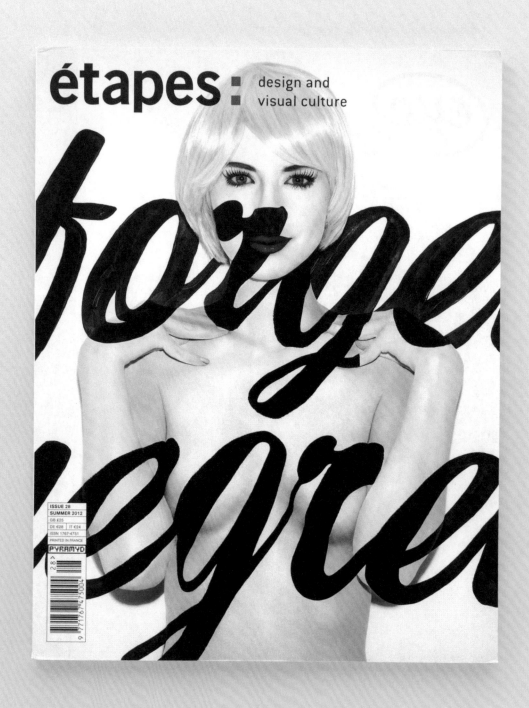

étapes
Country: France

Cover Design:
Michel Chanaud, Jean Loup Fusz

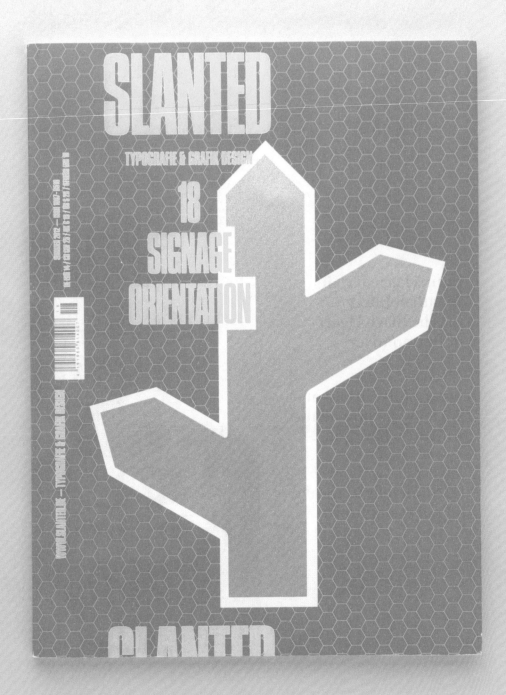

Slanted
Country: Germany

Art Direction:
Flo Gartner, Lars Harmsen

Studio

Issue Two ____ Autumn 2012

Browns ____ London, United Kingdom

Emma Parnell visits Jonathan Ellery in 'The Black Heart of Bermondsey'.

Genevieve Allison ____ New York, USA

Apparently Brooklyn is a lot nicer now all the wild dogs have gone.

Pentagram ____ Austin, TX, USA

DJ Stout tells us to take off our headphones.

Studio
Country: New Zealand

Cover Design: Clem Devine, Zoe Ilkin, Sam Trustrum

BAUHAUS

Die Zeitschrift der Stiftung Bauhaus Dessau
Ausgabe 4, Dezember 2012, 8 EUR
The Bauhaus Dessau Foundation's magazine
Issue 4, December 2012, 8 EUR

FOTO

Gertrud Arndt, Herbert Bayer, Marcel Dzama, T. Lux
Feininger, Werner David Feist, Gottfried Jäger, Will
Grohmann, Hannes Meyer, László Moholy-Nagy, Cord
Riechelmann, Rolf Sachsse, Thomas Walther, Umbo…

PHOTO

Automatisieren, digital denken, entwickeln, konservie-
ren, neu sehen, porträtieren, reproduzieren, sammeln,
tapezieren, überblicken, verbildlichen…
Automisation, digital thinking, developing, conserving,
new ways of seeing, portraying, reproducing, collecting,
wallpapering, reviewing, visualizing…

BAUHAUS DESSAU

Cover Design: Matthias Kreuzer,
Our Polite Society, Jens Schildt

Neshan
Country: Iran

Cover Design: Meshki Studio

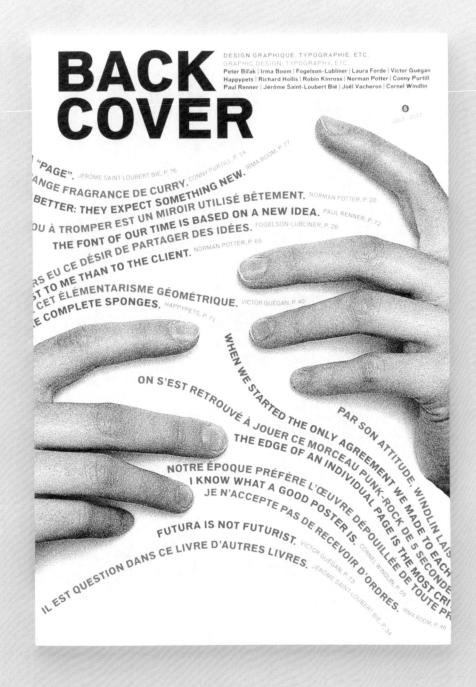

BACK COVER

DESIGN GRAPHIQUE, TYPOGRAPHIE, ETC.
GRAPHIC DESIGN, TYPOGRAPHY, ETC.

Peter Biľak | Irma Boom | Fogelson-Lubliner | Laura Forde | Victor Guégan
Happypets | Richard Hollis | Robin Kinross | Norman Potter | Conny Purtill
Paul Renner | Jérôme Saint-Loubert Bié | Joël Vacheron | Cornel Windlin

2012   2013

"PAGE". JÉRÔME SAINT-LOUBERT BIÉ, P. 76
ANGE FRAGRANCE DE CURRY. CONNY PURTILL, P. 14
BETTER: THEY EXPECT SOMETHING NEW. IRMA BOOM, P. 77
OU À TROMPER EST UN MIROIR UTILISÉ BÊTEMENT. NORMAN POTTER, P. 20
THE FONT OF OUR TIME IS BASED ON A NEW IDEA. PAUL RENNER, P. 72
RS EU CE DÉSIR DE PARTAGER DES IDÉES. FOGELSON-LUBLINER, P. 26
ST TO ME THAN TO THE CLIENT. NORMAN POTTER, P. 65
CET ÉLÉMENTARISME GÉOMÉTRIQUE. VICTOR GUÉGAN, P. 40
E COMPLETE SPONGES. HAPPYPETS, P. 71

WHEN WE STARTED THE ONLY AGREEMENT WE MADE TO EACH
ON S'EST RETROUVÉ À JOUER CE MORCEAU PUNK-ROCK DE 5 SECONDE
THE EDGE OF AN INDIVIDUAL PAGE IS THE MOST CRI
PAR SON ATTITUDE, WINDLIN LAI

NOTRE ÉPOQUE PRÉFÈRE L'ŒUVRE DÉPOUILLÉE DE TOUTE PR
I KNOW WHAT A GOOD POSTER IS. CORNEL WINDLIN, P. 59
JE N'ACCEPTE PAS DE RECEVOIR D'ORDRES. VICTOR GUÉGAN, P. 73

FUTURA IS NOT FUTURIST. IRMA BOOM, P. 46
IL EST QUESTION DANS CE LIVRE D'AUTRES LIVRES. JÉRÔME SAINT-LOUBERT BIÉ, P. 34

CLOG
Country: USA

Cover Design: CLOG

Creative Review
Country: UK

Art Director: Paul Pensom

Eye
Country: UK

Art Direction: Simon Esterson.
Cover image: Brian Denyer
(RCA Film Society, 1963)

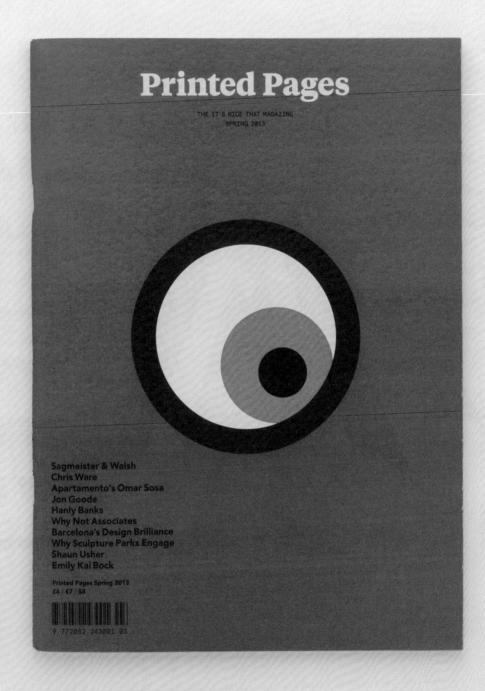

Printed Pages

THE IT'S NICE THAT MAGAZINE
SPRING 2013

Sagmeister & Walsh
Chris Ware
Apartamento's Omar Sosa
Jon Goode
Hanly Banks
Why Not Associates
Barcelona's Design Brilliance
Why Sculpture Parks Engage
Shaun Usher
Emily Kai Bock

Printed Pages Spring 2013
£4 / €7 / $8

9 772052 243001 03

THE CREATIVE REVIEW **ANNUAL**

In association with iStockphoto

Creative Review
Country: UK

Cover Photography: Marcus Ginns
Cover Design: Studio Myerscough

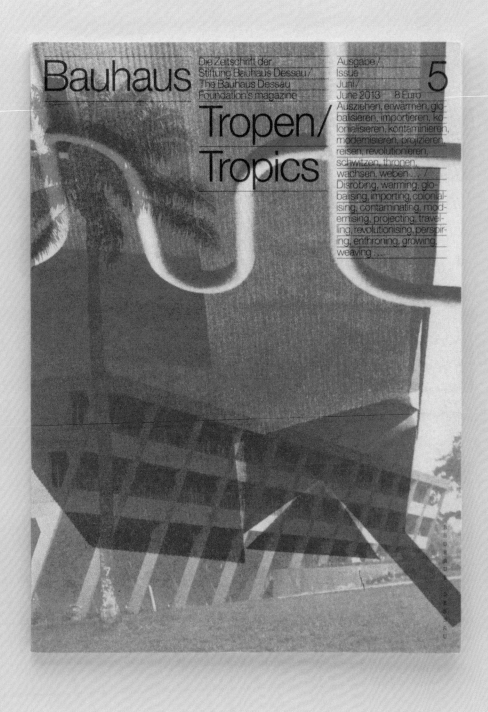

Bauhaus

Die Zeitschrift der
Stiftung Bauhaus Dessau /
The Bauhaus Dessau
Foundation's magazine

Tropen/
Tropics

Ausgabe /
Issue
Juni /
June 2013   8 Euro

5

Ausziehen, erwärmen, glo-
balisieren, importieren, ko-
lonialisieren, kontaminieren,
modernisieren, projizieren,
reisen, revolutionieren,
schwitzen, thronen,
wachsen, weben... /
Disrobing, warming, glo-
balising, importing, coloniali-
sing, contaminating, mod-
ernising, projecting, travel-
ling, revolutionising, perspir-
ing, enthroning, growing,
weaving ...

310

Wallpaper*
Country: UK

Photographer: Paolo Roversi
Cover Artist: Linder Sterling

AAfiles

67

AA Files
Country: UK

Cover Design: John Morgan Studio

Q How would you describe *MAS Context* (2009–present, USA)?

A *MAS Context* is a quarterly design journal that addresses issues that affect the urban context. Each issue explores a single topic through contributions from people working in different fields who provide different perspectives. Each issue is also an opportunity to collaborate with a new graphic designer who brings his or her point of view to the journal's design guidelines. Besides the print publication, we organise many public events to expand topics beyond the magazine and engage with new audiences. The content is always free, to make it accessible to everyone, regardless of economic means. In the end, *MAS Context* is a vehicle for sharing relevant proposals, ideas and experiences that help advance the way we think about our built environment.

Q What were the design and architectural magazines that influenced you when you started *MAS Context*, and what about any non-design/architecture magazines that impressed you?

A More than other magazines, the beginning of *MAS Context* was prompted by a previous experience of publishing a book. The structure was similar: focus on a single topic, contributors from different disciplines, and a combination of personal and academic essays with photographs and infographics. However, unlike that early experience, with *MAS Context* there was an opportunity to experiment with different collaborations and control how and when things were published. But there are magazines and publishers that I enjoy and that I think shaped my approach to publishing: early books by ACTAR, Lars Müller, Steidl, the publications of OMA/AMO (1978–present, various publishers), *COLORS* (1991–present, Italy), *Apartamento* (2008–present, Spain), *306090* (2002–present, USA). I am interested in publications that go beyond individual disciplines and take into consideration the production value.

Q What is the role of the contemporary magazine/journal looking at architecture and the built environment?

A I think that it is observing the world around us, being able to provide a sharp perspective about what is important, and ultimately finding ways to communicate why those aspects matter to a wide spectrum of people, not just designers. That doesn't mean that the content has to be dumb, but it also doesn't have to be presented as an impenetrable academic essay. Sometimes photo essays, brief comments or diagrams can communicate an idea more successfully. Topics and contributions can focus on what is important, not be driven by what the latest news is or by outside factors. It is a vehicle for the editorial team and contributors to share what they think has value. I like to think that our issues, while being published quarterly, don't have an expiry date so can be revisited years later, and remain as current as when they were initially published.

Q Historically, which are the most important US architectural magazines – and which non-US ones do you admire?

A I studied architecture in Spain, where I was exposed to publications such as *El Croquis* (1982–present, Spain) from Madrid and the publisher Gustavo Gili in Barcelona which have defined generations of architects. *Domus* (1928–present, Italy), founded by Gio Ponti, and *Abitare* (1961–present, Italy), are also well-established references in European architecture. Then there are the nine (and a half) pamphlets put together by Archigram from 1961 to 1974 that were the founding element of the group and a way to share their experimental ideas. They have been highly influential in architecture, serving as inspiration to younger generations. During my education I was less exposed to US publications, but *Oppositions* (1973–84, USA), or *Pamphlet Architecture* (1977–present, USA) have been influential in shaping the ideas and careers of prominent figures in the field.

Pamphlet Architecture
1977—present
USA

Q How would you categorise the state of architectural/environmental journalism today – bearing in mind the dominance of the Internet as an unregulated space for commentary and critique?

A Outside of the main commercial publications, I think there are a lot of interesting publications these days, whether in print, online or both. Now it is easier to work with authors and designers around the world and share your perspective on topics with anybody. People are experimenting with formats, bringing remarkable content from hidden archives, rediscovering interesting figures from the past and sharing work from emerging talent, and I think that is great. There is a lot of interesting content that deserves to be published. How to fund all these independent efforts might be another story.

Iker Gil is an architect, urban designer, teacher, director at MAS Studio, and Editor-in-Chief of its quarterly publication, MAS Context *– a magazine where each issue focuses on a single subject and addresses it from a range of design disciplines.*

MAS Context
2009—present
USA

Issue 20 / Winter 13
NARRATIVE

MAS Context
Country: USA

Art Direction: Plural
Cover Design: Chris Ware

Concrete Flux
Country: China

Cover Design: Solveig Suess

archphoto 2.0   holiday houses 03

plug_in

Archphoto 2.0
Country: Italy   Cover Design: Artiva Design

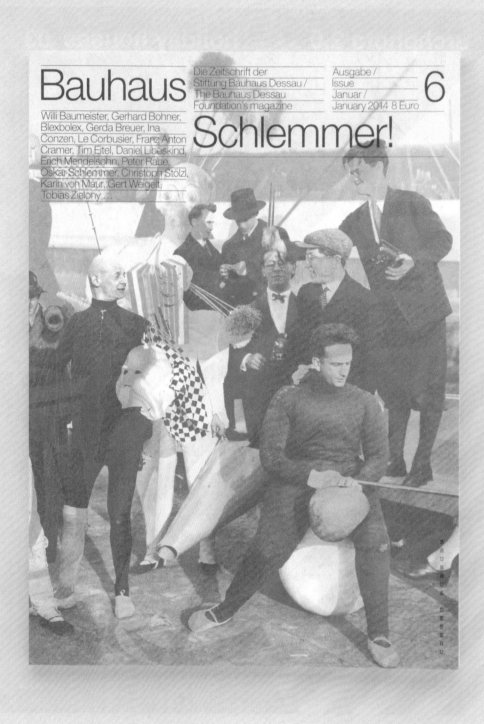

Bauhaus

Die Zeitschrift der
Stiftung Bauhaus Dessau /
The Bauhaus Dessau
Foundation's magazine

Ausgabe /
Issue
Januar /
January 2014 8 Euro

6

Willi Baumeister, Gerhard Bohner,
Blexbolex, Gerda Breuer, Ina
Conzen, Le Corbusier, Franz Anton
Cramer, Tim Eitel, Daniel Libeskind,
Erich Mendelsohn, Peter Raue,
Oskar Schlemmer, Christoph Stölzl,
Karin von Maur, Gert Weigelt,
Tobias Zielony . . .

Schlemmer!

Bauhaus
Country: Germany

Design: cyan

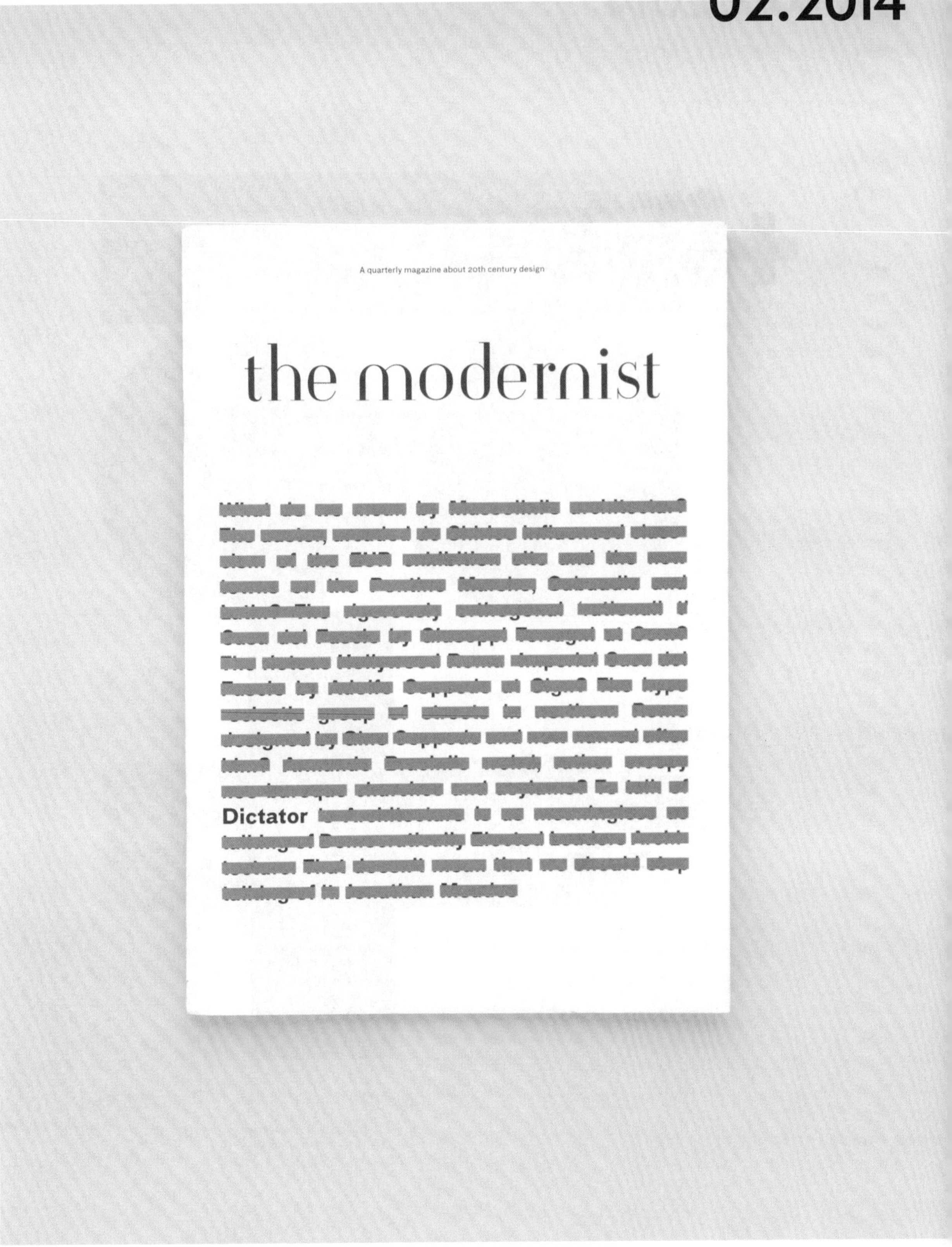

A quarterly magazine about 20th century design

the modernist

Dictator

Cover Design: Thomas Ulrik Madsen

PLUS EIGHTY ONE CREATORS ON THE LINE

VOL.63 / SPRING 2014
Book Design issue

/ BOOK
CREATORS
/ INDEPENDENT
PUBLISHERS
/ BOOK
SELLERS
PICTURE
BOOKS

+81
Country: Japan

Cover Design: Neville Brody

03—05.2014

Eye
Country: UK

Cover photograph: Lee Funnell
Art Director: Simon Esterson

321

Concrete Flux
Country: China

Cover Design:
Sophie Dyer, Solveig Suess

Printed Pages

The It's Nice That Magazine
Championing Creativity Across the Art and Design World
SPRING 2014

Lotta Nieminen · Andrea Aranow · Modern Toss
Aitor Throup · Tavi Gevinson and Minna Gilligan
Richard Turley · Stanley Donwood

9 772052 243018 03

£5 / €9 / $14

Process Journal
Edition Ten

Essay
Jeffrey Ludlow (2x4)

Features
2x4
Triboro
RoAndCo
Commercial Type

In conversation with
Eddie Opara & Natasha Jen
(Pentagram)

$25.00 USD
ISSN 1837–7807

Process Journal
Country: Australia

Art Direction & Design:
Thomas Williams

Slanted
Country: Germany

Art Direction:
Flo Gartner, Lars Harmsen

People of Print   Print Isn't Dead   Element #001

PRINT IS DEAD

Print Isn't Dead
Country: UK

Cover Design: Andy Cooke

WHEN THE CHIPS ARE DOWN: AN EXPO SPECIAL ON LIFE INSIDE THE WORLD'S MOST WELL-APPOINTED JAIL

MONOCLE

A BRIEFING ON GLOBAL AFFAIRS, BUSINESS, CULTURE & DESIGN

issue 76 . volume 08
SEPTEMBER 2014

(A) AFFAIRS Law and borders: on patrol in Paraguay's drug bandit territory

(B) BUSINESS It's a stick-up: a bamboo scaffolder's secrets

(C) CULTURE Ad creatives on the economy of words

(D) DESIGN Made in Italy: a heel-to-head tour of the nation's fashion-producing towns

(E) EDITS Marcio Kogan's well-designed last meal and Helsinki's market manoeuvres

ENTREPRENEURS GUIDE →

The New Entrepreneurs – and how you can join their ranks

Finish the plan, find the funding and finally do the thing you love. Learn how in **MONOCLE'S ANNUAL GUIDE** *to the changing world of good work*

In a year's time I want to be featured in Monocle's guide
1) Better stop reading this newspaper and get moving
2) Research my beard-care concept store
3) Keep my idea secret at all times

FOOD
How Good Eggs cracked the home-delivery business in the US

ADVICE CORNER
'In business relationships no good deed ever goes unnoticed' – send flattering, personal, purposeful email introductions

GROOMING
How some Greek busy bees created a beauty brand winner

LOGISTICS
How Munich's Carpooling is driving the sharing economy

FASHION
How inexperience created a hit shoe brand

SHALL WE BEGIN?

SERIAL THRILLER:
How to create a host of hit companies

THIS MUCH I KNOW:
Business owners on failure, success and the bits in between

10 INSPIRATIONAL COMPANIES:
From bicycle book deliveries to Paris property visionaries

LONDON · ZÜRICH · ISTANBUL · HONG KONG · TOKYO · TORONTO · NEW YORK

The Good Business GAZETTE

GLOBAL EDITION

Thursday 31 August | 2014
A Newspaper for Entrepreneurs from the founder of MONOCLE

+SARAWAK SUPPLEMENT
Our 28-page guide to Malaysia's rising region – and the challenges ahead

HEADLINES

All the ingredients for an Aussie success
How cookwear company Phillip&Lea created a rural retail haven where quality rules and profits gently rise

① **Let's start again:**
Revealed: The secrets of dusting off an old brand for a new generation

② **Hit the right note:**
How reinventing the keyboard kickstarted a harmonious company

③ **The new share deal:**
Why fresh work environments help to create good business

Dish of the day: Lisb
Inside the resta empire of José A

'Dream bigger – earlier'
Exclusive! Top tips from wise entrepreneurs

Creative Director: Richard Spencer Powell
Art Director: Emma Chiu
Design Director: Yoshitsugu Takagi

Concrete Flux
Country: China

Cover Design:
Solveig Suess, Sophie Dyer

Concrete Flux
Country: China

Cover Design:
Solveig Suess, Sophie Dyer

PIN—UP

Magazine for
Architectural Entertainment
Issue 17
Fall Winter 2014/15
USD 20.00

Featuring

Mario Botta
Sou Fujimoto
Kelly Wearstler
Kulapat Yantrasast
Carla Juaçaba

and Wolfgang Tillmans's
Book for Architects

ISSN 1933-9755

Norway

Mies Crown Hall
Americas Prize

Specials

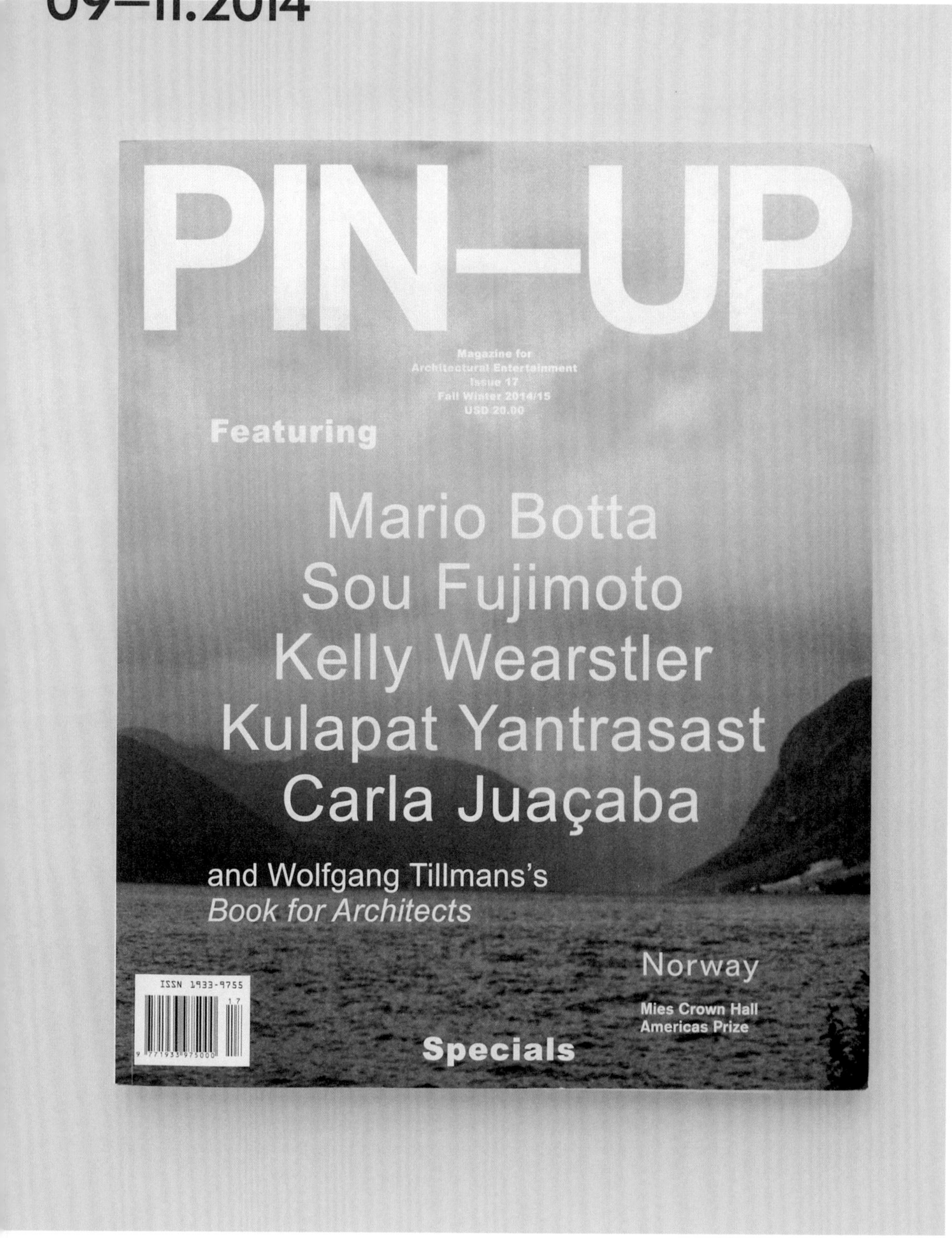

PIN—UP
Country: USA

Creative Director: Felix Burrichter
Design Director: Dylan Fracareta

BACK COVER
バックカバー

DESIGN GRAPHIQUE, TYPOGRAPHIE, ETC.
GRAPHIC DESIGN, TYPOGRAPHY, ETC.
All Right Graphics | Edo | Fukushima | Kazunari Hattori
Koga Hirano | Tohl Narita | Norakuro | Jan Tschichold
Yūichi Yokoyama | Bunpei Yorifuji, etc.

NUMÉRO SPÉCIAL JAPON
JAPAN SPECIAL ISSUE

Ce qui apparaît comme constant,
c'est la continuité de la présence d'un monde extérieur
au-delà des mers. Toshiaki Koga, p. 42
Je veux troubler le lecteur.
manipulating elements of letters. Yui Takada, p. 65
old people. Koga Hirano, p. 118
o reflect on the definition of good design, too few
ople approach the issue with criticism.
Satoshi Kondo, p. 125

Je travaille comme si j'avais
un mobile entre les mains.
Kazunari Hattori, p. 20 The day
I began keeping a diary all my anxieties disappeared.
Yūichi Yokoyama, p. 105 My heart was trembling
at the idea that I was about to meet the
creator of so many monsters.
Noi Sawaragi, p. 91

de vie des moines au temple.
u de ça. Yūichi Yokoyama, p. 24
f a blue figurine,
my eye. Alexandre Dimos, p. 90 At the outset,
japanese was a language with no writing.
Toshiaki Koga, p. 107

ai découpé dans un reprint
? Koga Hirano, p. 56
-être surpris que le créateur d'Ultraman
une maison aussi minuscule?
p. 6 The first time my brother Yui
ing press,
loveat first sight.
p. 121

Même pour l'observateur le plus déterminé,
le Japon ne se livre pas facilement.
The first word that comes into my mind Alexandre Dimos, p. 1
to describe the beauty of literary works in
Au Japon, la « révolution de l'imprimé » modern Japan is *yawaraka*.
ne passa pas par une invention technique, Minoru Niijima, p. 126
mais par le recours à un procédé ancestral. Christophe Marquet, p. 49
L'originalité japonaise du modèle
avant-gardiste de Tschichold reste, en grande partie, un mystère.
Victor Guégan, p. 46 After the war, Tagawa Suihō was criticised
for having encouraged militarism in young people
through his *Norakuro* stories. Isao Shimizu, p. 131
Haven't we all at some stage
felt like taking our lives? Bunpei Yorifuji, p. 96

Studio
Country: New Zealand

Cover Design: Clem Devine,
Zoe Ikin, Sam Trustrum

THE MODERN MODERNIST EXPO THE MODERNIST

MODERNIST

The Modernist
Country: UK

Cover Design: Thomas Ulrik Madsen

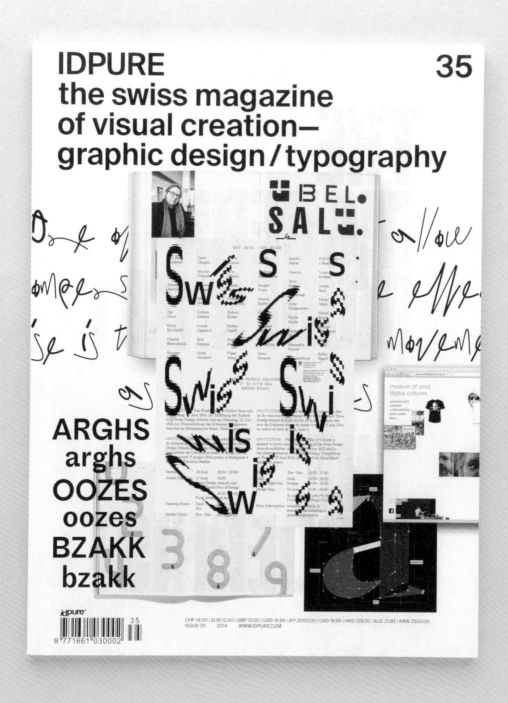

IDPURE
Country: Switzerland

Cover Design: Raphael Verona

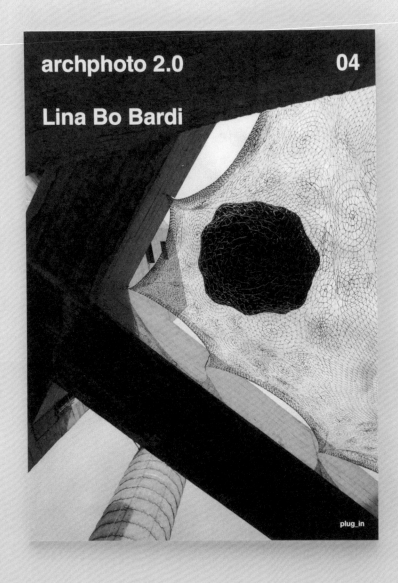

archphoto 2.0
Country: Italy

Cover Design: Artiva Design

Print Isn't Dead
Country: UK

Cover Design: Heretic Studio

Creative Director: Thierry Häusermann
Conception: This is Not
Design: Raphael Verona

Monocle
Country: UK

Creative Director:
Richard Spencer Powell
Art Director: Emma Chui
Desgn Director: Yoshitsugu Takagi

PIN–UP

Magazine for
Architectural Entertainment
Issue 18
Spring Summer 2015
USD 20.00

Featuring

David Adjaye
Tatiana Bilbao
Kunlé Adeyemi
SO–IL

with Justin Barry, Stephen Burks,
Frida Escobedo, DIS, Miguel Fisac,
Mame-Diarra Niang, Valerio
Olgiati, Adam Pendleton, Anders
Ruhwald, Atang Tshikare

CARNET
D'AFRIQUE
BY
IWAN BAAN

ISSN 1933-9755

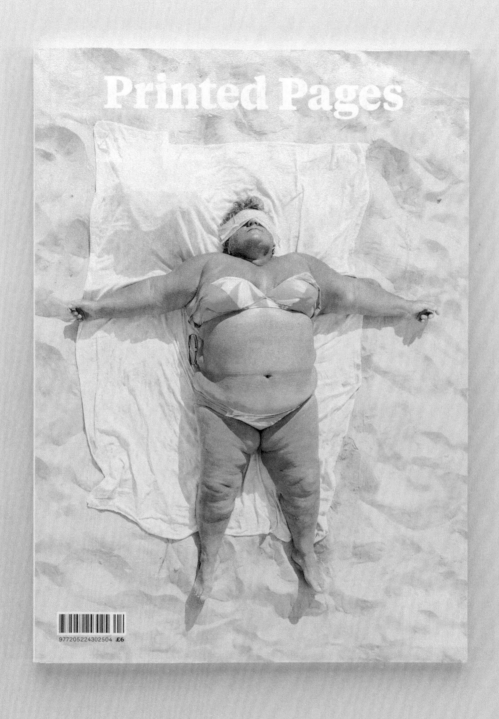

Printed Pages
Country: UK

Cover Design: Tadao Cern

slanted 25   25 × 25

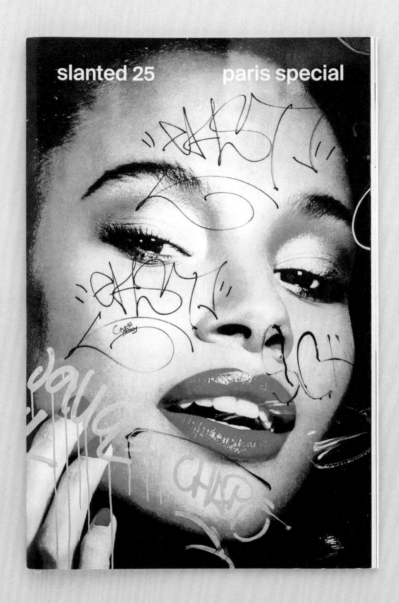

Slanted
Country: Germany

Art Direction: Lars Harmsen

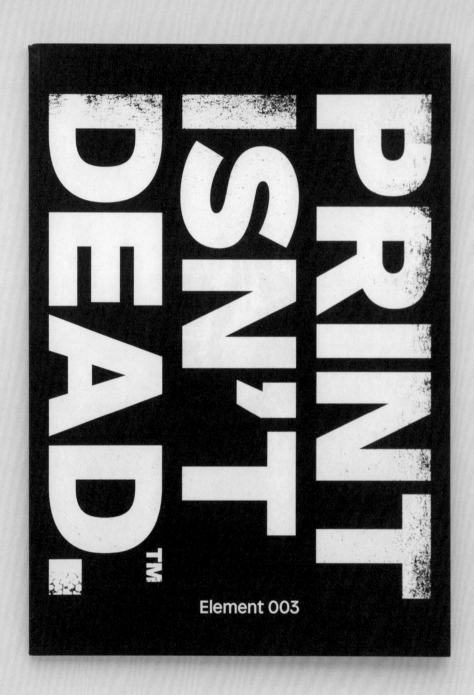

Print Isn't Dead
Country: UK

Cover Design: James Lunn

Creative Director: Thierry Häusermann
Conception: This is Not
Design: Raphael Verona

BRAND.
BALANCE.

BRAND
DOCUMENTARY
MAGAZINE

ISSUE NO.37
TSUTAYA

B

TSUTAYA

ENG. KRW 16,000

B
Country: South Korea   Cover Design: Younghyun Ok

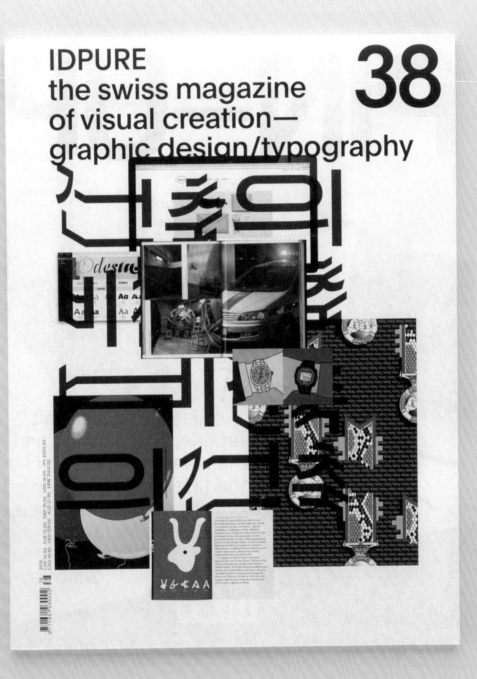

IDPURE
Country: Switzerland

Creative Director: Thierry Häusermann
Conception: This is Not
Design: Raphael Verona

PIN–UP

Featuring
Jean Nouvel, Ippolito
Pestellini Laparelli,
Wendy Goodman, Pedro
Friedeberg, Trix and
Robert Haussmann,
Ugo Rondinone,
Yrjö Kukkapuro,
Luca Cipelletti, and
MOS Architects

MAGAZINE FOR
ARCHITECTURAL
ENTERTAINMENT
ISSUE 19

THE GREAT INDOORS

Plus
Jessi Reaves, Soft
Baroque, Toshiko Mori and
Tomas Maier, Candida Höfer,
Carmen Herrera, Avery Singer,
Mickalene Thomas, Kaari Upson,
Sahra Motalebi, Lena
Henke, and Diane
Simpson

ISSN 1933-9755

Fall Winter 2015/16

USD 30.00

PIN–UP
Country: USA

Creative Director: Felix Burrichter
Art Direction & Design: Erin Knuston

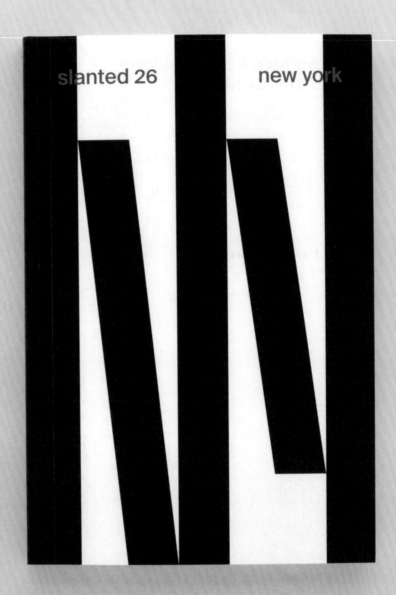

slanted 26   new york

Slanted
Country: Germany   Art Direction: Lars Harmsen

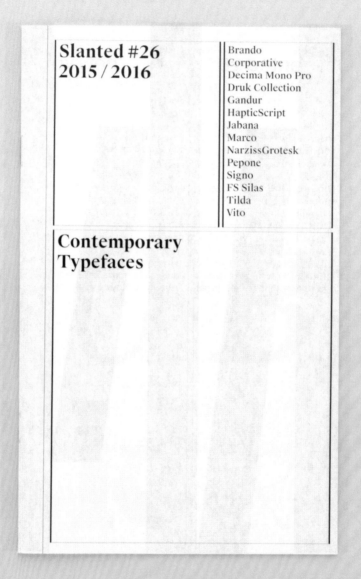

Slanted #26
2015 / 2016

Brando
Corporative
Decima Mono Pro
Druk Collection
Gandur
HapticScript
Jabana
Marco
NarzissGrotesk
Pepone
Signo
FS Silas
Tilda
Vito

Contemporary
Typefaces

Slanted
Country: Germany

Art Direction: Lars Harmsen

Concrete Flux
Country: China

Cover Design:
Solveig Suess, Sophie Dyer

Neshan
Country: Iran

Cover Design: Meshki Studio

Observer Quarterly
Country: USA
Creative Director: Jessica Helfand

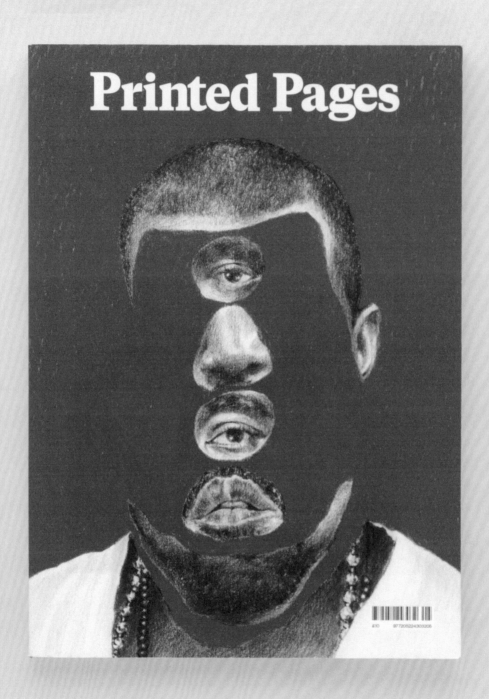

354

Printed Pages
Country: UK

Cover Design: Eric Yahnker

Q What was the first design publication that gained your attention – and why?

A When I started my foundation year at Bournville (near Birmingham) I often referenced a book called *Pen & Mouse* (2001). I can't remember exactly how I found it but it was my first introduction to people like Ian Wright, Jasper Goodall and Kate Gibb. It was one of those books that really opened my eyes to what design and illustration was. It was around the same time that I discovered Magma's online store and bought a few magazines. One of these was *Graphic* which I think preceded *Elephant* magazine (2009-present, UK), run by Marc Valli (who also runs Magma). Again, it just opened up a world of creatives and a sense of knowing that I was reading the right thing.

Q It's Nice That is seen as an online success story in design publishing. But you also have a print arm. The online version is free, but the printed version has to be paid for – how does this affect your thinking regarding content?

A It's changed a lot over the years as we've tried to get to grips with it (I think we're probably still working it out if we're honest). The way we currently look at it is that content is the really important thing, good content, and that is what we strive to produce. When we have it, we want to share it with as many people as possible, so everything we currently do has an online life. We believe people are increasingly likely to read a 1000-plus-word article online, either at their desktops or on their mobiles, or to save it to read later on apps like Pocket. What we prioritise is making content available and allowing people to share it.

When it comes to print we then do an edit of what we consider to be the most interesting content from the last six months and publish it biannually through *Printed Pages* (2013–present, UK). What changes here is the way in which it's presented and the way in which people engage with it. What we believe you have to do in print now is either create something very cheap and disposable or create something special and something people will want to keep and refer back to – we opted for the latter. We can also add an incentive to online sales by offering exclusive or limited edition prints and collateral.

Q *Printed Pages* – starting with its name – seems to embody a commitment to print. Do you think you will still be publishing a printed magazine in five years' time?

A Who knows? I'm as excited by the question of whether we will still have an online platform in five years' time. The biggest thing I've learnt in the last nine years is to be open to change and to embrace it. We currently have a viable print offering that has an audience, and a model that makes it an enjoyable and profitable thing to do. This hasn't always been the case with the print products we've published, and why we've stopped some things and changed others. If I had to take an educated guess I'm pretty sure people will still be buying magazines in five years' time, and I'd hope we'd still be able to publish something people are keen to read.

Q Can you say something about the cover designs for *Printed Pages*? Are they designed with the newsstand in mind?

A 65% of the copies we publish end up on the newsstand, so it is one of the many things we take into consideration. I'd love to say there's more that goes into it, but the truth is it's more often than not a gut feeling, either an image or an idea, and something we feel proud to put out. With hindsight we've probably learnt a lot from the covers we've published in the past, but it's still one of toughest parts of the process.

Q Can you name some contemporary design publications that you admire?

A The acid test for me now is can a magazine that is over its honeymoon period, and the excitement of launching, consistently produce a publication that I'm excited about buying. There are a lot of excellent launch issues that never reach a third and fourth issue. Also, buying has become an important part to consider in this. We are lucky that we get sent a lot of magazines at It's Nice That and it's often not an honest reflection of the magazine – it's very

Printed Pages
2013—present
UK

easy to say something's good when you've not had to part with your own cash.

The magazines that I buy within a week of them coming out are *The Gentlewoman* (2010–present, UK), for its writing and design. *The Gourmand* (2011–present, UK) for its attention to detail in a physical product. *Elephant* (2009–present, UK) for the coverage of a very specific sector of the art world. *Eye* (1990–present, UK) magazine I still really like for the in-depth design writing. *Saturdays Magazine* (2012–present, USA) for its big, glossy take on surf culture. *Apartamento* (2008–present, Spain) for its dedication to a printed thing as the only way to read the content. *Popeye* (1976–present, Japan), just to look at and take it all in. The one that probably breaks the rule as it's only three issues into a new era after recently being bought is *Holiday* magazine (1946–1977, USA, Relaunched 2014, France), for its unabashed size that makes it almost impossible to take anywhere, but which it more than makes up for in the stories and commissioning. I'm sure I've missed someone obvious out.

Will Hudson co-founded It's Nice That as a university project in 2007, and has overseen its growth to include a website, creative agency and printed magazine.

Bauhaus Ausgabe 7 ~~Kollektiv~~

Die Zeitschrift der
Stiftung Bauhaus Dessau
Dezember 2015, 12 Euro

9 783959 050586

BAUHAUS DESSAU

Bauhaus
Country: Germany

Design: Prill Vieceli Cremers

Lifestyle ◆ Architecture ◆ Objects

150 ISSUES!
New
mission
New
attitude

ICON

◆
Design
worth
knowing
◆

Special relaunch edition

One hundred and fifty issues — and a brand new look

ISSUE 150
DECEMBER
2015

UK £5.00
EUR €9.99
USA $13.99

BONUS
150 things
worth knowing
16-page
supplement

Bringing
Albania back
to life
Can architecture
save the day?

Gothenburg
and its sci-fi sauna
+ Oslo
has a new bar by
Anderssen & Voll

PLUS
Kit worth craving
Hotel Tivoli
Inside the Ozeki
factory in Gifu

Icon
Country: UK

Art Director: Anja Wohlström
Design: Simon Kühn

359

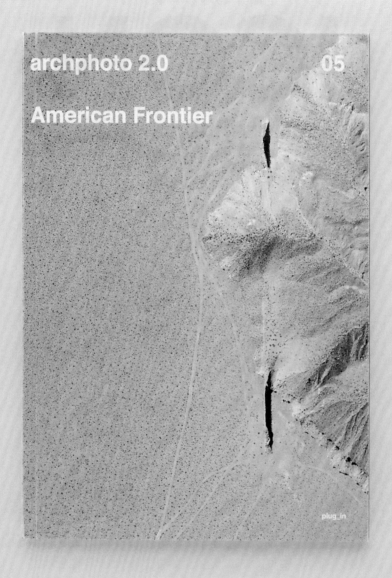

archphoto 2.0   05

American Frontier

plug_in

Archphoto
Country: Italy

Cover Design: Alessandro Lanzetta

Print Isn't Dead
Country: UK

Cover Design: Jon Bland

Disegno

The Quarterly Journal of Design #10
Spring 2016

This issue includes: *Jasper Morrison's* memories of Tsukiji fish market; 13 ghosts of Milan's past; the fictitious femmes of *Erdem*; *Jane Thompson* on mid-century design journalism; *Felipe Ribon's* necro-functionalism; *Sanaa* and the utopia of transparency; *OMA* in conversation about the perils of preservation; and Pritzker Prize-winner *Alejandro Aravena* explaining the theme of the 2016 Venice Architecture Biennale.

p.97 Reflections on Transparency

p.145 The Spectre of Milan

p.113 19th-century Modern

UK £8 US $19

10>

9 772048 777022

Disegno
Country: UK

Creative Directors:
Florian Böhm, Annahita Kamali

Slanted
Country: Germany

Art Direction: Lars Harmsen

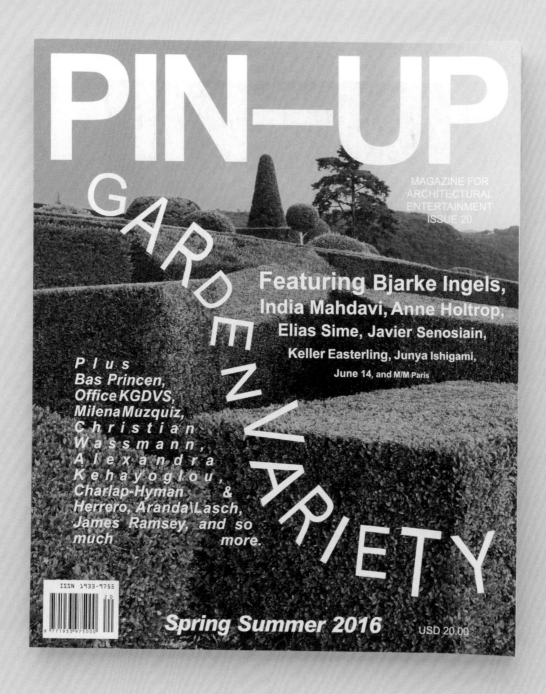

PIN–UP

MAGAZINE FOR
ARCHITECTURAL
ENTERTAINMENT
ISSUE 20

GARDEN VARIETY

**Featuring Bjarke Ingels,
India Mahdavi, Anne Holtrop,**
Elias Sime, Javier Senosiain,
Keller Easterling, Junya Ishigami,
June 14, and M/M Paris

*Plus
Bas Princen,
Office KGDVS,
Milena Muzquiz,
C h r i s t i a n
W a s s m a n n ,
A l e x a n d r a
K e h a y o g l o u ,
Charlap-Hyman   &
Herrero, Aranda\Lasch,
James Ramsey, and so
much   more.*

ISSN 1933-9755

Spring Summer 2016   USD 20.00

PIN–UP
Country: USA

Creative Director: Felix Burrichter
Art Direction & Design: Erin Knutson

Lifestyle ◆ Architecture ◆ Objects

ICON

T R A V E L

Transported by Design
London's tube network gets a makeover

Ben van Berkel
Stations, bridges and luxury towers

Y-3 goes galactic
Designing a stylish spacesuit

China Rail Revolution
Impact of high-speed on a nation

Designing the Hay way
Founders reveal route to success

ISSUE 154
APRIL 2016
UK £5.00
EUR €9.99
USA $15.99

Lo Res Lamborghini
United Nude revamp the ultimate car

Kodak's Super 8 Camera
Yves Béhar brings analogue back

Bento Boxes
Lunch on the go, from kawaii to cool

The fast lane
Tearing down the Autobahn

9 771479 945024

04>

Icon
Country: UK

Art Director: Anja Wohlström
Design: Simon Kühn

365

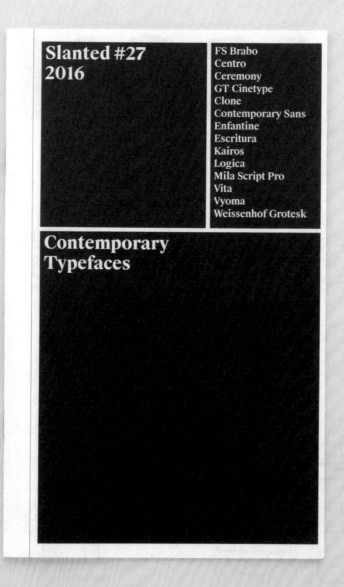

Slanted #27
2016

FS Brabo
Centro
Ceremony
GT Cinetype
Clone
Contemporary Sans
Enfantine
Escritura
Kairos
Logica
Mila Script Pro
Vita
Vyoma
Weissenhof Grotesk

Contemporary
Typefaces

Slanted
Country: Germany

Art Direction: Lars Harmsen

Slanted
Country: Germany

Art Direction: Lars Harmsen

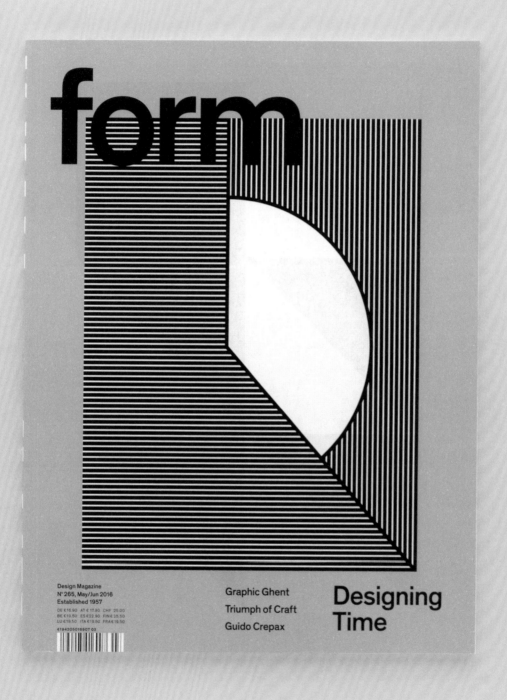

form
Country: Germany

Cover Design: Studio Studio

Monocle
Country: UK

Creative Director:
Richard Spencer Powell
Design Director: Yoshitsugu Takagi

369

Eye
Country: UK

Art Director: Simon Esterson
Cover image: sanitation worker,
Memphis, 1968

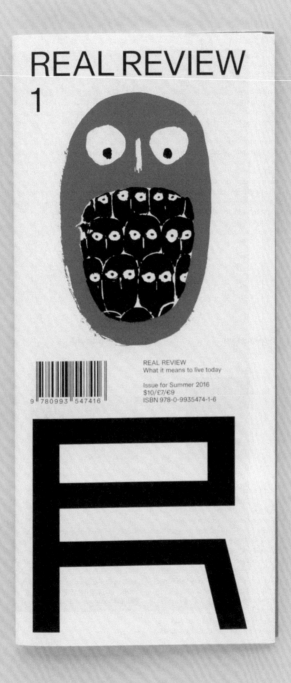

Real Review
Country: UK

Cover Illustration: Nishant Choksi
Cover Design: OK-RM

The publications

+81 (1997–present, Japan) is a Tokyo-based quarterly magazine covering graphic design, fashion, film, music and creative activities around the world. Each issue is devoted to a single theme. Recent subjects have included brand architecture, photography and designer John Warwicker. All articles are presented in both Japanese and English. In addition to the magazine, the +81 group runs a concept gallery (+81 Gallery+Lab) and an independent publishing label (+81 Publishing). It also hosts a creative conference called Tokyo Graphic Passport. Cover design for the issue shown here is by Neville Brody.

AA Files (1981–present, UK) is the Architectural Association School of Architecture's journal of record, and the successor to a long line of house journals that began with the school's founding in 1847. The journal appears twice a year and offers 'writerly models of scholarship, criticism and investigation, prompted not only by work, exhibitions and events from within the school, but by a rich and eclectic mix of architectural enquiry from all over the world'. Design is by John Morgan Studio. The editor is Thomas Weaver.

AD (*Architectural Design*) (1930–present, UK) is a UK-based architectural journal first launched as *Architectural Design and Construction*. Between 1946 and 1975, the editor was Monica Pidgeon, a notably progressive and influential figure in the world of architecture. The owners at that time, however, did not like the fact that *AD* had a female editor, and to 'reassure' readers and advertisers they insisted that male architects' names were placed on the masthead as 'consultants'. Pidgeon was a supporter of Buckminster Fuller and numerous articles on Fuller's work appeared in the pages of *AD*. In the late 1970s and 1980s the journal became a voice for postmodern architecture.

Adbusters (1989–present, Canada) is the brainchild of Estonian-born documentary filmmaker Kalle Lasn, and is an entirely advertising-free, not-for-profit publication produced by a network of writers, artists and activists. Its content is designed to challenge the commercial forces that shape psychological, physical and cultural environments. The Adbusters Media Foundation was formed after successful anti-consumerist, pro-environment activism, and this in turn led to the founding of *Adbusters* magazine. It began as a local quarterly with three full-time volunteers and a circulation of 5,000, and is now an international bi-monthly, with a dozen editors, over 250 freelancers and a circulation of 120,000.

AJ (*Architects' Journal*) (1895–present, UK) was originally named *The Builders' Journal and Architectural Record*. Between the years 1906 and 1910 it was known as *The Builders' Journal and Architectural Engineer*, and then in 1911 it was renamed *The Architects' and Builders' Journal*. In 1919 it adopted its current name, since when it has been at the heart of British architecture, covering projects from small builds to the development of cities, and providing critical opinion across the breadth of the industry. It was redesigned in 2005 by APFEL (pp. 223). In 2014 the magazine ceased to be a print publication and went online.

AR (*The Architectural Review*) (1896–present, UK) has been published continually since 1896. It is one of the world's leading monthly architecture magazines, and covers topics such as landscaping, interior design and urban planning. Described by architecture critic Deyan Sudjic (pp. 095) as 'the grand old lady of architectural publishing', its covers have been designed by many important British graphic designers including Philip Thompson and Brian Stapely.

archphoto 2.0 (2011–present, Italy) is an open-access, peer-reviewed magazine. It began life as an online publication, but was re-launched as a magazine in 2011, and acts as the print arm of its original web presence – archphoto.it. The magazine serves as a critical review of the practice of architecture viewed within the context of today's visual culture. Subjects covered include the architecture of Palm Springs, inflatables and disco. The black and white design is by Artiva Design, a multi-disciplinary studio based in Genoa, Italy, and working in graphic design, branding and visual communication.

Back Cover
2008—present
France

Back Cover (2008–present, France) is a French publication focusing on graphic design and typography. The magazine describes itself thus: '*Back Cover* does not deal with news and does not present portfolios. It contains thoughts, critical or historical analysis and individual or collective experiences in graphic design, typography, illustration and visual arts.' Recent issues have featured articles on Herbert Spencer (No.2), Metahaven (No.4) and Japan (No.6). *Back Cover* is published by B42, an initiative set up by the Paris studio deValence. Formed by Alexandre Dimos in 2001, the studio designs books, visual identity, signage and websites for a variety of clients.

Baseline
1979—present
UK

Baseline (1979–present, UK) began life under the ownership of Letraset, as a vehicle to promote new typeface designs. The first issue was designed and edited by Mike Daines. In 1993 Hans Dieter Reichert became the magazine's art director, working alongside Daines. But dispite a healthy subscriber list, a growing reputation for good content and a developing relationship with internationally known writers, Letraset relinquished its interest in the publication and in 1995 Hans Dieter Reichert and Mike Daines became the owners. Today it is owned by Hans Dieter Reichert and designed by HDR Visual Communication. It is best known for its wrap-around poster covers and its in-depth coverage of typography and type design.

Bauhaus
1926—present
Germany

Bauhaus (1926–present, Germany) is the journal of the Bauhaus Dessau Foundation. The first issue of the magazine was published to coincide with the opening of the Bauhaus building in Dessau in 1926. The publication continued until 1931 when it ceased publication. But, 80 years after its discontinuation, Bauhaus Dessau Foundation returned with a new magazine under the old name. They say: 'we by no means presume to replicate an interrupted tradition ... Nonetheless, it does work at the same place – the Bauhaus building in Dessau – and its remit is to cultivate the legacy of the historic Bauhaus.' The *bauhaus* magazine is published twice a year. Design is by Cyan.

Blueprint
1983—present
UK

Blueprint (1983–present, UK). The architectural writer Peter Murray saw the need for a magazine that combined strong photography with critical analysis. Architecture critic Deyan Sudjic was appointed as *Blueprint*'s first editor, and Simon Esterson was appointed as art director. The magazine adopted the use of striking photographic portraits of 'star' architects and designers, a feature that distinguished it from other architecture publications of the period. A team of young writers were hired, including Jonathan Glancey, James Woudhuysen, Rowan Moore and Rick Poynor. Sudjic continued to edit *Blueprint* until 1994. Past editors have included Rowan Moore, Marcus Field and Vicky Richardson. Art directors have included Andrew Johnson, John Belknap and Patrick Myles. The magazine recently underwent a major redesign under current editor Johnny Tucker.

B
2001—present
South Korea

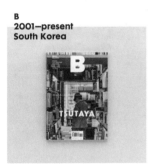

B (2001–present, South Korea) is an ad-free monthly publication that in each issue introduces what they term a 'well-balanced brand unearthed from around the globe'. It continues: '*B* pursues its quest for true value of a printed medium by becoming a magazine that would be worth possessing, not affected by advertisements since it receives no financial support from the brand, and maintains a unique and independent perspective which is increasingly disappearing due to overflowing information mingled among different media outlets.' Subjects covered include Leica, Penguin and the record label ECM.

Circular
1993—present
UK

Circular (1993–present, UK), is the house journal of the Typographic Circle, 'a social club which brings together anyone with an interest in type and typography'. Since issue 8 (1999), the publication has been designed by Pentagram partner Domenic Lippa. To date, 18 issues have appeared. Under Lippa's direction, *Circular* carries no advertising and is not sold on newsstands. This gives him the freedom to be experimental. He says: '*Circular* should ultimately feel like someone has cared for it – which we do. It should be a platform for different points of view and should not choose sides but allow the members the opportunity to see and read about great work. This is a totally pro bono project for both the editorial and design sides of the project and therefore only comes out every 18 months'.

CLOG
2011—present
USA

CLOG (2011–present, USA) is an international publication that 'critically explores one topic at a time from as many perspectives as possible'. This small format, perfect-bound 'mook' is now in its 15th issue. The edition shown here is devoted to Brutalism. Amongst numerous articles, it features a reprint of Reyner Banham's famous essay 'The New Brutalism', first published in *The Architectural Review*, 1955.

Concrete Flux
2013—present
China

Concrete Flux (2013–present, China) describes itself as 'a multi-media, multi-disciplinary journal which takes as its subject matter China's hyper-fast emerging urban spaces, their meaning and one's everyday experiences of them'. It began life as an online journal before publishing its first printed issue in 2013. They say: 'We believe that a new configuration of space through urbanisation will lead to a new configuration of society. Our aim, then, is to contribute to some understanding of or gain insight into what these spaces, which seem to emerge faster than our minds can log and assess, may mean.'

Creative Review
1981—present
UK

Creative Review (1981–present, UK) emerged during the 1980s design boom, and has been a major presence in British design and advertising ever since. Its distinctive square format and glossy pages are regularly restyled to reflect current design thinking. Throughout its time it has embraced new media, and has a strong web and social media presence. The magazine covers graphic design, digital media, typography and visual communication, and in recent issues has expanded its field of vision to include topics such as health, travel and transport, food and drink. The current editor is Patrick Burgoyne, and the art director is Paul Pensom.

Da!
1994—95
Russia

Da! (1994–95, Russia) was a short-lived but influential publication. Due to conflict with the owners (a Russian advertising agency) over editorial independence and the commercial prospects of the magazine, the fifth and final issue of *Da!* was self-published by the magazine's editors Vladimir Krichevsky and Elena Chernevich. Krichevsky is a designer, art historian, collector and author and designer of numerous graphic design publications. Elena Chernevich is the author of *Russian Graphic Design, 1880–1917*. The magazine had a determinedly international outlook with issues devoted to such subjects as Dutch design.

Design
1959—77
Japan

Design (1959–77, Japan), was subtitled A Quarterly Review of Design, and published by Bijyutsu Shuppan sha. Along with *Idea* and *Graphic Design*, it was one of the three most important Japanese design journals in the post-war period. *Design* covered a wider range of topics including industrial design, product design, environmental design and occasionally, graphic design. The issue shown here features articles on the paintings of Josef Müller-Brockmann and his Japanese wife Shizuko Yoshikawa, and on American orange crate labels.

Design Issues
1984—present
USA

Design Issues (1984–present, USA) was the first American academic journal to examine design history, theory and criticism. The journal promotes academic inquiry into cultural and intellectual issues surrounding design. Regular features include theoretical and critical articles by professional and scholarly contributors, extensive book and exhibition reviews. Special guest-edited issues concentrate on particular themes, such as design history, human-computer interface, service design, organization design, design for development, and product design methodology. *Design Issues* is published online and in print by MIT Press. Cover design for issue shown here is by Ken Hiebert.

Design Quarterly
1954—93
USA

Design Quarterly (1954–93, USA). The first 28 issues of this magazine were published by the Walker Art Center, under the title *Everyday Art Quarterly*. In 1954, the magazine became *Design Quarterly*. With issue 159 (1993), the Walker Art Center ceased its affiliation with the journal, and it was briefly owned by MIT Press. *Design Quarterly* charted the design landscape in America, from contemporary architecture and product design to a more focused look at the social impact of design. Issue 63 (1965) was guest-edited by Reyner Banham. Graphic Design did not feature prominently until the editorship of Mildred Freeman (1972–91), when it featured more frequently. In the 1980s issues were guest-edited by, amongst others, Armin Hofmann, Wolfgang Weingart and April Greiman.

Design+Design
1984—unknown
Germany

Design+Design (1984–unknown, Germany) began in 1984, and was originally named *Braun+Design*. This was changed to *Design+Design* from issue 21 onwards. It is subtitled Independent Magazine for Design Collectors. The publication lasted for 96 issues. Most issues had text in English and German. The magazine featured articles devoted to subjects such as Braun headphones, desk fans and toasters; products produced at the firm's Barcelona plant; a celebration of the Model 214 chair by Thonet (on its 150th birthday); and features on other 'milestone' Braun designs. Issues are highly sought after today by Braun collectors.

Disegno
2011—present
UK

Disegno (2011–present, UK) was founded by Johanna Agerman Ross as a biannual dedicated to in-depth and critical writing around architecture, design and fashion. In 2016 *Disegno* became a quarterly publication and was redesigned by Florian Böhm and Annahita Kamali of Studio AKFB. Each cover of the magazine receives a different visual treatment, while *Disegno*'s logo exists in two fonts – Tiempos and National.

DNI
2007—present
Argentina

DNI (2007–present, Argentina) is a quarterly magazine carrying national and international design news. *DNI* stands for (Diseño Internacional y Nacional – International and National Design). It is a publication of Clarín, the largest newspaper in Argentina, published by the Grupo Clarín media. The issue shown contains articles on typography, furniture, vehicle design and sports shoes.

Domus
1928–present
Italy

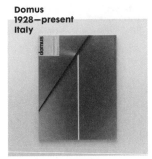

Domus (1928–present, Italy) was founded by architect Gio Ponti to ignite interest in architecture, interiors and Italian design. A monthly magazine, *Domus* has been a leading publication since its inception in 1928. Over the years its remit has increased to cover industrial design, advertising graphics and digital communications, with a more international focus. Gio Ponti was the first editor; Deyan Sudjic was editor between 2000 and 2004. *Domus* published its thousandth edition in 2016.

Dot Dot Dot
2001–11
UK/Netherlands

Dot Dot Dot (2001–11, UK/Netherlands) was a deceptively modest-looking publication that marked a sea change in design publishing. Initially covering purely graphic design, *Dot Dot Dot* expanded to include articles on language, music, film and literature. Doggedly anti-commercial, it was closer to various art and literature publications than it was to graphic design journalism. Founded by Stuart Bailey and Peter Bil'ak, *Dot Dot Dot* exemplified the notion that graphic design was no longer a discipline that needed to justify its existence. After ten years and twenty issues it ceased publication in 2010.

Emigre
1984–2005
USA

Emigre (1984–2005, USA) was a hugely influential US-based publication, established by Rudy VanderLans and Zuzana Licko. It was launched in the same year as the Apple Mac, and is widely regarded as the first publication of the computer era. *Emigre* embraced the flexibility of the new digital modes of working, and regularly changed its format and typefaces. Along the way it went from a tabloid format to a paperback book to a music CD. In addition, it caused controversy both through its written content and its radical stylistic shifts. Writers included Andrew Blauvelt, Mr. Keedy, Lorraine Wild, Kenneth FitzGerald and Rick Poynor. Emigre exists today as a respected type foundry.

étapes
1994–present
France

étapes (1994–present, France) is published bi-monthly, and intended for graphic design and visual communication professionals. It offers readers a wide-ranging view of both French and international graphic design, industry news and opinion. The magazine is edited by Isabelle Moisy and Caroline Bouige. Versions exist for Android and Ipad. The text is in French.

Eye
1990–present
UK

Eye (1990–present, UK) was launched under the editorship of writer Rick Poynor. The magazine announced itself as a quarterly journal devoted to international graphic design. Poynor saw it as 'informed, thoughtful, sceptical, literate, prepared to take up a position and argue a case'. Under his editorship, *Eye* became widely regarded as evidence of graphic design's growing maturity as a discipline. Poynor left the editorship in 1997, and was succeeded by Max Bruinsma. The current editor and proprietor, John L Walters, took over in 1999. The current art director (and co-owner with Walters) is Simon Esterson, who has art-directed the magazine since issue 58.

form
1957–present
Germany

form (1957–present, Germany) was founded as *International Revue* by Jupp Ernst, Willem Sandberg, Curt Schweicher and Wilhelm Wagenfeld. *Form* started as a wide-ranging cultural magazine dealing with art, architecture and industrial design, but also discussing ballet, music, poetry and designer manifestos. What began life as the idea of four creative people in 1957 is today a forum offering topics that are intended to 'stimulate the design discourse'.

Form+Zweck
1956–unknown
Germany

Form+Zweck (1956–unknown, Germany) translates as Form and Purpose. Originally published as *Form und Zweck* (1956–90), this East German publication was founded by the Institute of Applied Arts to document and develop professional design work. Its editors, as employees of the East German government, could not express ideas that were not government sanctioned, and any articles that supported consumerist or capitalistic leanings were censored. But after the fall of the Berlin Wall the journal was commercially reformulated as *Form+Zweck*.

Format
1968–1980
Germany

Format (1968–c.1980, Germany) was subtitled Zeitschrift für verbale und visuelle Kommunikation (the magazine of verbal and visual communication). It covered advertising, PR, communication in writing and image, and was published six times a year. It carried articles on typography and photography, and often featured inserts from the paper industry. It was founded by designer and art director Hubertus Carl Frey. Publisher and editor-in-chief for many issues was Dieter Gitzel.

Fuse
1991–unknown
UK

Fuse (1991–unknown, UK) was launched by Neville Brody and Jon Wozencroft as a guerrilla publication that for twenty issues vigorously challenged typographic formalism and championed the new digital technology. Published quarterly, each issue was constructed around a theme, and four designers were invited to produce a typeface and a poster. Fonts were loaded onto floppy discs and packaged in a brown cardboard box. The first eighteen issues included a diskette of original fonts and posters by a variety of designers, including Malcolm Garrett, Peter Saville, Matthew Carter, Cornel Windlin, David Carson, Tibor Kalman, Barry Deck, Paul Elliman, Tobias Frere-Jones and Bruce Mau.

FUTU
2007–present
Poland

FUTU (2007–present, Poland) is a magazine about 'design, art and trends in luxury'. The publication is designed by various leading European design studios, and has won numerous awards for its design. The version shown here is about brands, and is designed by the leading magazine designer Matt Willey. It is published by the Publishing and Design Group, Warsaw, with both Polish and English text.

Grafik
2003–present
UK

Grafik (2003–present, UK) has its origins in a 1980s publication called *Hot Graphics International*. The magazine was subsequently transformed under editor Tim Rich into the monthly publication *Graphics International*. In 2001 Caroline Roberts took over editorship and in 2003, now called *Grafik*, the magazine underwent a radical transformation. In 2011 it ceased to be a print publication and exists today as an online platform for designers, critics and influencers in visual culture. The website is updated daily with industry news, design history and long-form critical articles. It is edited by Caroline Roberts and Angharad Lewis.

Graphic
2003–2009
UK

Graphic (2003–09, UK) described itself as a 'contemporary graphic culture magazine.' It was founded by Marc Valli, co-owner and founder of Magma, the highly respected mini-chain of bookshops specialising in art and design books, magazines and related material. According to Valli, *Graphic* 'never found its feet as a magazine proper, and ended up as more of a book series, with every issue looking at one theme in particular. Making a whole magazine on just one theme can be tricky. Sometimes a theme works, and the issue sells, sometimes it doesn't, and then..." Graphic was replaced by Elephant, the art and visual culture magazine, with Valli as Editor-in-Chief.

Graphic
2007–present
South Korea

Graphic (2007–present, South Korea) works on a one-issue, one-theme basis. It is an independent magazine published in South Korea and focuses on alternative and outsider trends in graphic design. After graduating in 2008 from Arnhem's Werkplaats Typografie, Na Kim designed and edited the magazine between 2009 and 2011. Recent issues have been devoted to subjects such as Dutch printers and graphic designers, young studios, book shops and computational design.

Graphic Design
1959–86
Japan

Graphic Design (1959–86, Japan) was edited by designer Masaru Katsumi, *Graphic Design* was one of Japan's most significant design magazines, showcasing both Japanese designers alongside Western counterparts. It lasted for exactly 100 issues. According according to *Idea* editor Kiyonori Muroga, 'Masaru was an agent for change, developing the quality and social position of Japanese graphic design. In post-war Japanese society, *Graphic Design* was a vehicle to develop and establish the high cultural standard of graphic design. The content was very curated and academic, compared with other magazines.'

Graphis
1944–present
Switzerland

Graphis (1944–present, Switzerland) was first published in 1944, in Zürich, Switzerland by Walter Herdeg and Walter Amstutz. After a split from Amstutz in 1964, Herdeg became the sole publisher. The company was sold in 1986 to B. Martin Pedersen, and the headquarters were relocated to New York. *Graphis* has been a hugely influential showcase for graphic design, advertising and illustration since its launch. It continues today, with over 350 issues published.

Hard Werken
1978–82
Netherlands

Hard Werken (1978–82, Netherlands) was formed by a group of Rotterdam graphic designers. Two years later they formed themselves into Hard Werken Design, a loosely structured cooperative group with membership that included Gerard Hadders, Henk Elenga, Tom van der Haspel, Rick Vermeulen and Willem Kars. They were formed without a dogma, and rejected the prevailing trends and fashions. The collagist design of the magazine exemplified the founders' anarchic anti-formalistic approach, and included articles on experimental typography, photography and illustration.

IDPURE
2004–present
Switzerland

IDPURE (2004–present, Switzerland) is a quarterly magazine describing itself as 'the Swiss magazine of visual creation – graphic design/typography'. It offers a comprehensive picture of creativity in Switzerland and beyond, and claims to provide a 'source of information, inspiration and expression'. The magazine's website announces that a 'less scholarly' version of *IDPURE* is in preparation, and at 192 pages it will be 'closer to a book' than a magazine. Instead of publishing four issues a year it will offer a double edition twice a year.

Icographic
1971–78
UK

Icographic (1971–78, UK) was edited and designed by Patrick Wallis Burke. The magazine was designed on a four-column grid with headings in Helvetica and body copy in Univers Medium. It was published quarterly by ICOGRADA (International Council of Graphic Design Associations) as an academic journal that attempted to bring visual communication design research to a wider international audience. ICOGRADA was founded in 1963 in London, by Peter Kneebone and Willy de Majo, to create meaningful international dialogue around the future of graphic design. ICOGRADA is known today as ico-D, and publishes the journal *Communication Design*, Interdisciplinary and Graphic Design Research, led by editor-in-chief Teal Triggs.

Icon
2003–present
UK

Icon (2003–present, UK) is a leading architecture and design magazine. It states that 'every month the most exciting architects and designers in the world are interviewed, the best new buildings are visited, the most interesting new cultural movements and technologies are analysed and an eclectic range of exhibitions, books, products and films are reviewed. Beautifully presented and accessible, rigorous and insightful, *Icon* shows what's happening in architecture and design today, and what it means for the future.'

IdN
1992–present
Hong Kong

IdN (1992–present, Hong Kong) is aninternationally focused publication intended to bring together the design community in the Asia-Pacific region and showcase their work in – as the name suggests – 'an international designers' network'.

Idea
1953–present
Japan

Idea (1953–present, Japan) remains one of the most important and longstanding graphic design publications in the world. It has been at the forefront of the international graphic design scene since its inception. Initially the magazine functioned as a shop window for designers around the world. In more recent years, and now under the editorship of Kiyonori Muroga, the magazine has developed a more critical position. *Idea* has always made high-grade reproduction and state-of-the-art printing two of its defining qualities. This is coupled with striking covers and a dynamic non-formatted layout.

Industrial Design (I.D.)
1954–2009
USA

Industrial Design (I.D.) (1954–2009, USA) was the invention of publisher Charles Whitney. He was persuaded by his friend the designer George Nelson that a specialised periodical devoted to the growing field of industrial design was needed. Alvin Lustig was the first art director. Many covers in the late 1960s were done by Massimo Vignelli. The print magazine closed in 2009. By this time it was known as *I.D.*, whose editors included Ralph Caplan, Chee Pearlman and, lastly, Julie Lasky.

Inventario
2010–present
Italy

Inventario (2010–present, Italy) is supported by the Italian lighting manufacturer Foscarini. The title refers to the idea that making an inventory to gather and put into order what is in front of us is the best way of deciphering and understanding what is around us. On its masthead the magazine uses the slogan 'Tutto è progetto/Everything is a project.' The magazine describes itself as 'midway between a book and a magazine' and 'aims to cast a critical eye over the design scene by looking at all design disciplines.' Shown here is issue No.4, which carries an article on Italian graphic designer Leonardo Sonnoli.

Kyoorius
2006–present
India

Kyoorius (2006–present, India) is published by a non-profit organisation which aims to connect the creative community in India. An initiative by Transasia Fine Papers Pvt Ltd, the Kyoorius brand comprises an annual conference (Kyoorius Designyatra) and a magazine (*Kyoorius*). The bi-monthly magazine focuses on showcasing the most promising work being produced in Indian graphic design, branding and advertising, with the aim of bringing India's fast-evolving visual culture to an international audience.

Lecturis Documentaire
1974—2011
Netherlands

MAS Context
2009—present
USA

The Modernist
2011—present
UK

Monocle
2007—present
UK

Lecturis Documentaire (1974–2011, Netherlands) is a series of publications produced by Lecturis, the Dutch publisher and (formerly) printer. Founded in 1922 as a publishing company, printing became its primary activity from 1940 onwards. In 2015, the printing activities of Lecturis were taken over by Wilco Art Books, and today the company's main focus is publishing books on art, photography and design. The *Lecturis Documentaire* series is devoted to investigating themes in graphic design. Prominent individuals involved in the series include: Wim Crouwel, Paul Mijksenaar, Hard Werken, Jurriaan Schrofer and Mevis and Van Deursen. Issue 12 (shown here), deals with the emergence and development of graphic design at the Hague Academy in the 1930s.

MAS Context (2009–present, USA) is a quarterly journal from Chicago-based architecture and urban design firm Mas Studio: both were founded by Iker Gil. The magazine was launched to address issues that affect the urban landscape by engaging in debate and participation from different design fields on a single topic per issue. It states: 'Our approach is simple and profound. Each issue asks people to think of new possibilities. Leading all of us to collaborate in new ways. This unleashes a great debate. And asks designers everywhere to act in new and unimagined ways.' Themes tackled to date include Information (No.7), Surveillance (No.22) and Legacy (No.25/26). Design is by leading Chicago design studio Thirst.

The Modernist (2011–present, UK) is a quarterly publication devoted to 20th-century modernist architecture and design. Published by the Modernist Society, based in Manchester, UK, it contains 'news, reviews, musings and delightful titbits about modernist architecture and design'. According to *The Morning Star*, *The Modernist* 'valiantly champions 20th-century architecture'. Edited by Jack Hale and Emily Gee, it is designed by Thomas Ulrik Madsen. The Society's patrons are Jonathan Meades and Johnny Marr.

Monocle (2007–present, UK) was founded by journalist Tyler Brûlé as a defiantly print-based enterprise, launched at a time when print was under sentence of death from electronic publishing. *Monocle* is a magazine briefing on 'global affairs, business, culture and design'. It describes itself as the 'complete media brand with our print, audio and online elements – not to mention our expanding retail network and online business'. The distinctive art direction is by Richard Spencer Powell.

Neshan
2003—present
Iran

novum
1971—present
UK

OASE
1981—present
Netherlands

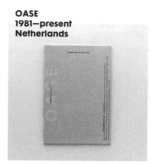

Observer Quarterly
2015—present
USA

Neshan (2003–present, Iran) was founded by leading figures from Iran's design community: Majid Abbasi, Saed Meshki, Morteza Momayez, Ali Rashidi, Firouz Shafei and Iraj Zargami. Majid Abbasi is the magazine's editor-in-chief. He says: 'Our aim in publishing *Neshan* is to introduce Iranian graphic design to our community and to the graphic designers in other countries and cultures. At the same time, we decided to cover both contemporary graphic design and the past graphic art in Iran and the world. We decided to introduce the great masters of the twentieth century which had not been done on such a scale in Iran before.'

novum (1971–present, UK) has for eighty-five years tracked design activity in Germany and across the world. Between 1971 and 1996 it was known as *novum-gebrauchsgraphik*, and before that as *Gebrauchsgraphik*. The magazine presents articles on contemporary practitioners such as Stefan Sagmeister and Karlssonwilker. Published by Stiebner Verlag in Munich, *novum* has a monthly circulation of 13,500 in over 80 countries.

OASE Journal for Architecture (1981–present, Netherlands) is published three times a year. The magazine's mission statement announces: '*OASE* is an independent, international, peer-reviewed journal for architecture that brings together academic discourse and the sensibilities of design practice. *OASE* advocates critical reflection in which the architectural project occupies a central position, yet is understood to be embedded in a wider cultural field.' The publication's fluid and ever-changing design is by Karel Martens and Werkplaats Typografie, Arnhem. The journal is published by NAi Publishers, Rotterdam by order of the OASE Foundation. To date 96 issues have been published.

Observer Quarterly (2015–present, USA) is a print offshoot of the influential design blog *Design Observer*. Issues are themed around specific topics such as 'sound', 'tagging' and 'food and drink'. Creative Director is *Design Observer* co-founder Jessica Helfand. After many years as an online-only presence, a *Design Observer* printed publication came as a surprise to many. As editor Eugenia Bell states: 'We believe in the word, the power of ideas in print, and the ephemerality, spontaneity, and fleetingness of them in periodicals. A magazine makes sense.' Three issues have appeared to date.

Octavo
1986—92
UK

Octavo (1986–92, UK). Eight issues of *Octavo* were edited, designed and published by the design group 8vo. The magazine's primary focus was typography. It took no advertising and was entirely self-financed. It was also a reaction against the way design in the 1980s had been 'hijacked by marketing men' (their phrase). The publication studiously avoided promotional activity of any kind and pursued a polemicised study of European asymmetric typography. The publication was also a *tour de force* of print production, involving advanced printing techniques. The eighth issue was published as an interactive CD-ROM.

PIN—UP
2006—present
USA

PIN-UP (2006–present, USA) has been described as the 'Playboy of architecture magazines'. It is a biannual publication, and proclaims itself as the only magazine for architectural entertainment. In its own words, '*PIN–UP* is a magazine that captures an architectural spirit, rather than focusing on technical details of design, by featuring interviews with architects, designers, and artists, and presenting work as an informal work in progress.'

Pamphlet Architecture
1977—present
USA

Pamphlet Architecture (1977–present, USA) was founded by architects Steven Holl and William Stout as a venue for publishing the thoughts and work of a younger generation of architects. Each issue was written, illustrated and designed by a single architect. *Pamphlet* invites practitioners and theorists to present their ideas in a manner that is as visually provocative as it is intellectually compelling. Geoff Manaugh of BLDGBLOG has noted: 'To this day, the pamphlet format – short books, easily carried around town, packed with spatial ideas and constructive speculations – remains inspiring.'

Print Isn't Dead
2014—present
UK

Print Isn't Dead (2014–present, UK) is a self-published magazine by People of Print. The magazine started life as a Kickstarter project. The title proved prophetic, as the project exceeded its original funding goal. Each issue is designed differently, with the intention of showcasing the vast and varied uses of print. The founder and editor is Marcroy Eccleston Smith, and design is by James Lunn.

Printed Pages
2013—present
UK

Printed Pages (2013–present, UK) was founded by the team at It's Nice That, bringing together a mix of art and design content. Published as a companion to the group's hugely popular website, *Printed Pages* is a bi-annual saddle-stitched publication featuring profiles, interviews, photo essays and texts. At the time of writing, issue 16 has just been published. It is described as 'an inspiring snapshot of the creative world curated by the It's Nice That team'. The issue shown here has 240 pages and is published with three different covers.

Process Journal
2007—present
Australia

Process Journal (2007–present, Australia) is a design publication by Made Publishers. It was founded by partners Thomas Williams and Amber Hourigan. The aim of the journal is not only to serve as a source of inspiration for designers and graphic designers alike, but also to investigate the 'process' behind influential creative work. Printed on high-quality uncoated stocks utilising a five-colour printing process, the journal comprises 100-plus pages of advertising-free content.

Projekt
1955—unknown
Poland

Projekt (1955–unknown, Poland) was one of the few publications in the Eastern Bloc to showcase the art and design not only from behind the Iron Curtain, but also from the West. Particularly striking were its covers, many of them created by members of the famous Polish Poster School – among them Henryk Tomaszewski, Józef Mroszczak and Jan Lenica. As a satellite state of the Soviet Union, Poland was subject to censorship and repression, and Polish artists and designers were expected to adhere to the official Soviet style of Socialist Realism. But Poland has a long history of rebellion and opposition, and this contrarian spirit can be seen in the pages and covers of numerous editions of *Projekt*.

Push Pin Graphic
1957—80
USA

Push Pin Graphic (1957–80, USA) began life as a publication sent to friends and clients by Seymour Chwast and Milton Glaser shortly after they started Push Pin Studios. It was first called *The Monthly Graphic*, but this soon changed to *Push Pin Graphic* (partly to disguise the erratic appearance of the magazine, and partly to identify it more closely with the Push Pin Studio). Later, when Push Pin Studios started to represent illustrators it became a highly effective promotional tool. The publication developed a dedicated following, eventually running for 23 years and 86 issues. Few designer-led publications can be said to have been more influential. It was a true pioneer.

Real Review
2016—present
UK

Real Review (2016–present, UK) is published by the Real Foundation, a cultural institution with a 'double mission of critical inquiry and cultural production'. It conducts original research to promote innovation in the built environment. *Real Review* covers subjects ranging from the housing crisis to mass-surveillance, and offers 'insightful, engaging reviews on architecture exploring how design shapes society'. Design is by OK-RM and the publication is edited by Jack Self.

Signes
1991—98
France

Signes (1991–98, France) was a graphic design magazine created by Michel Wlassikoff (Publishing Director), Frédéric Massard and Muriel Paris. Twenty-two issues were published between 1991 and 1998. In 2014, *Signes* was reactivated as a website focusing on graphic design and typography (www.signes.org). Michel Wlassikoff is the author of the authoritative book *Histoire du graphisme en France* (2005).

Slanted
2004—present
Germany

Slanted (2004–present, Germany) is a small-format typography magazine. It has been in existence since 2004, and was designed to complement the slanted.de website (launched in 2004). It is published bi-annually and each issue is dedicated to a different topic. The design of each issue of the magazine reflects these topics. Both blog and magazine encourage debate on the subjects of typography, graphic design, illustration and photography. Topics covered in *Slanted* include stencil type (No.9), signage (No.19) and slab serf (No.20). Whole issues have been devoted to design and typography from Switzerland (No.23), Istanbul (No.24) and Paris (No.25). Issues are intended to be collected as a reference work.

Studio
2011—present
New Zealand

Studio (2011–present, New Zealand) was created by three New Zealand-based designers (Clem Devine, Sam Trustrum and Zoe Ikin). *Studio* is an international magazine dedicated to profiling spaces belonging to creative practitioners of all kinds – from graphic designers to furniture makers, from architects to artists. As Zoe Ikin notes: 'It's interesting to see the kind of things designers and creative people surround themselves with. Their furniture, books and generally how they arrange their spaces.'

TYP
1986—unknown
Netherlands

TYP (Typografisch Papier) (1986–unknown, Netherlands) was edited and founded by Assi Koostra, Max Kisman and Peter Mertens, with the aim of 'rejuvenating the Dutch design and typography community' and 'declaring war on the state of design, typography and taste of the Dutch aesthetic elite.' The first edition was published in a transparent envelope. The size and format varied from issue to issue. Some editions came with a CD or CD-ROM. In 2012, the first edition of *TTYPP* (as the journal was now called) appeared as an app for the iPad.

Typographic
c.1960s—present
UK

Typographic (1971–present, UK) was founded by the International Society of Typographic Designers, itself founded in 1928 by Vincent Steer with the aim of developing the profession of typography in the UK. With six colleagues, Steer held the first meeting of the British Typographers Guild. Its name was changed in 1953 to the Society of Typographic Designers (STD) and then in 1999, recognising its influence in other countries, and at the request of then president Colin Banks, the name was changed to the International Society of Typographic Designers. In 1971, the society launched *Typographic*, the official ISTD journal. Under David Jury's editorship (1996–2006), the magazine grew in status and quality. It is distributed free to ISTD members.

Typographic-i
1977—85
USA

Typographic-i (1977–85, USA) was the journal of the US-based Typographers International Association (TIA). The -i stood for ideas, information, inspiration. The TIA was a trade organisation founded as the International Trade Composition Association in 1920, to represent the interests of typesetters and typesetting companies within the printing industry in the United States and Canada. In 1941 the organisation was renamed the International Typographic Composition Association, and in 1980 it took the name Typographers International Association. The magazine ran for 24 issues, and featured articles on typography and type history as well as book reviews.

Typographics Ti
1980—present
Japan

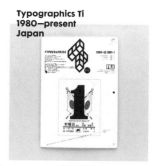

Typographics Ti (1980–present, Japan) was first issued in May 1980, as a quarterly periodical published by the Japan Typography Association, an organisation founded in 1965 and originally called the Japan Lettering Designers' Association. It was formed to further the development of typography in Japan, and to support designers and educators focused on the research and production of typography. They host a yearly awards programme. *Typographics Ti* is still published in Japan.

TM
1932–present
Switzerland

TM (Typographische Monatsblätter) (1932–present, Switzerland). Along with *Neue Grafik*, *TM* was one of Switzerland's two most significant graphic design journals. Published by Der Schweizerische Typographenbund (STB) in Bern, it played a crucial role in advancing modernist graphic design in Switzerland. Jan Tschichold was an important contributor. In the 1990s, *TM* championed the work of Wolfgang Weingart and other radical neo-modernist Swiss typographers. A book was published in 2013 by Lars Muller detailing the history of this important typographic journal titled, *30 Years of Swiss Typographic Discourse in the Typografische Monatsblätter.*

Typos
c.1980–82
UK

Typos (c.1980–82, UK) was subtitled *An International Journal of Typography.* *Typos* was edited by teacher and type designer Fred Lambert. First published in 1980 by the London College of Printing, the first issue featured articles on Total Design, Oliver Simon and Edward Johnston. Fred Lambert is best remembered as the designer of the Letraset typeface Compact. *Typos* lasted for six issues. (Thanks to UAL Archives and Special Collections Centre.)

U&lc
1970–99
USA

U&lc (1970–99, USA) was founded by Herb Lubalin and the International Typeface Corporation. *U&lc* (*Upper & Lower Case*) was a magazine for showcasing the graphic arts and typography, and under Lubalin's editorship it became a powerful voice in the phototypesetting world. It featured an eclectic mix of vintage and contemporary subject matter: an article by Norman Mailer on graffiti sits next to one on Spencerian script. Yet, despite the diversity of subject matter, *U&lc* was a commercial enterprise. ITC (of which Lubalin was a founder) used it as a platform to publicise their new typefaces. The tabloid-format publication appeared quarterly and was distributed by direct mail, free to anyone who signed up to receive it. By the end of the 1970s it had a controlled circulation of over 250,000 and an international readership, according to ITC, of one million.

Varoom
2005–present
UK

Varoom (2005–present, UK) is the journal of the Association of Illustrators (AOI), The magazine focuses on illustration, culture and society, and offers space for commentators to discuss and provide criticism on contemporary illustration. The magazine first appeared in 2005 as a perfect-bound A4 journal, edited by Adrian Shaughnessy and designed by Non Format. John O'Reilly took over the editorship in 2009 (*Varoom* 10). Design is by Studio Fernando Gutiérrez. Regular contributors include Marian Bantjes and Paul Davis. The magazine has undergone a number of format and design changes in recent years, and since its inception it has become an important voice in contemporary illustration.

Visible Language
1967–present
USA

Visible Language (1967–present, USA) is a peer-reviewed design journal, published by the University of Cincinnati, which investigates how visual communication can enhance the human experience. From an initial focus on typography, the journal evolved to reflect the changing landscape of communication design, and to embrace interdisciplinary relationships with subjects such as anthropology, art, design, education and linguistics. Founding editor Merald Wrolstad understood that research and scholarly information were essential to the development of communication design. In 1987, the journal passed to its second editor Sharon Poggenpohl, who strengthened the investigation of design research, interdisciplinary thinking and the evolution of digital communication, along with its cultural impact. The current editor is Mike Zender.

Wallpaper*
1996–present
UK

*Wallpaper** (1996–present, UK) was launched by journalist Tyler Brûlé as a publication for design conscious urbanites. In 1997 it was acquired by publishing conglomerate Time Warner, and under editor-in-chief Tony Chambers and creative director Sarah Douglas it has become a key publication in the international coverage of design, architecture, interiors, art, fashion and travel. The magazine is distinguished by its high-end photography and art direction. Bespoke covers and inserts are a regular feature of the magazine.

De vorm
1975–76
Netherlands

De vorm (1975–76, Netherlands) was a short-lived 28-page design journal featuring industrial design, graphic design, interior design and 'multiple art'. Only six issues were distributed before it ceased publication. It featured articles with a social and political bias. Typical of this was an interview with Jurriaan Schrofer about his role as consultant for the art works in the Amsterdam metro. At the time many people were critical of this project because it meant that a number of houses had to be demolished, and there were loud protests. The compact, no-frills, one-colour layout of the magazine was by the Dutch design studio Tel Design.

Vormberichten
1989–2013
Netherlands

Vormberichten (1989–2013, Netherlands) was published by the beroepsvereniging Nederlandse Ontwerpers (bNO) as the first of a series of printed newsletters called *bNO Nieuwsbrief* (bNO Newsletter). In 1990, the name was changed to *Vormberichten*, a combined publication by bNO and Kring Industriële Ontwerpers (KIO). In 2013, Vormberichten was discontinued and replaced by *Dude, Dutch Designers Magazine.* This new quarterly is available to non-members of BNO, and can be bought in Dutch book stores, online and as a subscription.

Editors' thanks

Impact 2.0, Design magazines, journals and periodicals [1974–2016], and it's sister publication *Impact 1.0, Design magazines, journals and periodicals [1922–73]*, have been made possible by the generosity and enthusiasm of the following institutions, publishers and individuals:

Archives (both volumes):

Rose Gridneff, the guardian of the University of the Creative Arts archive in Epsom, UK, not only gave us unfettered access to a vast collection of magazines, but also allowed us to draw from her personal collection. Sasha Tochilovsky, a long-standing friend of Unit Editions, gave us freedom to select specimens from the many international titles held at the Herb Lubalin Study Center of Design and Typography in New York, USA. The book was built around the foundation that these two archives provided.

Contributors (both volumes):

We owe a special debt of thanks to the following individuals who contributed magazines and journals from their personal collections: Seymour Chwast, Paula Scher (*Push Pin Graphic*); Rachel Dalton, Jack Grafton, Callin Mackintosh, Sam Stevenson, Tommy Spitters (Spin/Unit Editions); Sarah Douglas (*Wallpaper**); Richard Doust (RCA); Simon Esterson (Esterson Associates and *Eye*); Richard Hollis; Mark Holt (*Octavo*); Domenic Lippa (Pentagram); Matt Lamont (FoxDuo); Quentin Newark (Atelier Works); Richard Spencer Powell (*Monocle*); Hans Dieter Reichert (*Baseline*); Sascha Lobe (L2M3); Mason Wells (Bibliothéque).

Interviewees (both volumes):

James Biber (Biber Architects); Patrick Burgoyne (*Creative Review*); Kirsty Carter and Emma Thomas (A Practise For Everyday Life); Ken Garland; Iker Gil (*Mas Context*); Rose Gridneff (UCA), Richard Hollis; Mark Holt (*Octavo*); Will Hudson (It's Nice That); Jeremy Leslie (Mag Culture); Kiyonori Muroga (*Idea*); Hans-Dieter Reichardt (*Baseline*); R Roger Remington (Vignelli Centre for Design Studies); Caroline Roberts (*Grafik*); Paul Shaw; Deyan Sudjic (Design Museum); Teal Triggs (RCA); Rudy VanderLans (*Emigre*); Carlo Vinti (Progetto grafico); Mason Wells (Bibliothéque).

Publishers/rights owners (both volumes):

Satoru Yamashita (*+81*); Thomas Weaver (*AA Files*); Kalle Lasn (*Adbusters*); Jon Astbury (*AJ*); Emanuele Piccardo (*Archphoto*); Alexandre Dimos (*Back Cover*); Katrin Zbinden (*Bauen+Wohnen*); Johnny Tucker (*Blueprint*); Mondadori Group (*Casabella*); Sallyanne Theodosiou (*Circular*); Kyle May (*Clog*); Solveig Seuss (*Concrete Flux*); Patrick Burgoyne/Centaur Media (*Creative Review*), Design Council/University of Brighton Design Archives via Chris Finnegan (*Design*); Jo Klatt (*Design+Design*); Ashley Duffalo, Courtesy the Walker Art Centre (*Design Quarterly*); Johanna Agerman Ross (*Disegno*); Domus S.p.A (*Domus*); Peter Bilak, Stuart Bailey (*Dot Dot Dot*).

Rudy Vanderlans (*Emigre*); Michel Chenaux/Isabelle Moisy/Pyramyd (*Etapes*); John L. Walters (*Eye*); Peter Wesner/Stephan Ott (*Form*); Johnathon Vaughn Strebly (*Format*); Christine Moosmann, Hans Peter Copony/Stiebner Verlag GmbH (*Gebrauschgraphik & novum*); B Martin Pedersen (*Graphis*); Caroline Roberts/Grafik Ltd (*Grafik*); Kim Kwangchul (*Graphic*); Paul van Mameren/Lecturis (*Hard Werken*); Patrick Wallis Burke/The International Council of Graphic Design Associations (*Icographic*); John Jervis/Anja Wohlstrom (*Icon*); Kiyonori Muroga (*Idea*); Laurence Ng/Systems Design Limited (*IdN*); Thierry Häusermann (*IDPURE*); Sam Vallance, F+W (*Industrial Design/I.D.*); Maurizio Corraini Srl. (*Inventario*); Mike Zender (*The Journal of Typographic Research*); Iker Gil (*Mas Context*); © DACS 2016 (*Neue Grafik*); NAi Publishers/Karel Martens (*Oase*); Hamish Muir (*Octavo*).

Erin Cain (*Pamphlet Architecture*); Marcroy Eccleston Smith (*People of Print*); Felix Burrichter/FEBU Publishing (*Pin–Up*); Cody Lee Barbour (*Print Isn't Dead*); Zachary Petit (*Print*); It's Nice That (*Printed Pages*); Thomas Williams (*Process Journal*); Jack Self (*Real Review*); Michel Wlassikoff (*Signes*); Julia Kahl (*Slanted*); Domus S.p.A (*Stile Industria*); Studio (*Studio*), Paul van Mameren/Lecturis (*De maniakken*); Jack Hale (*The Modernist*); Observer Omnimedia LLC (*The Quarterly*); syndicom – Swiss union for media and communication (*TM*); Peter Mertens, Max Kisman (*TYP*); Jonathan Doney, International Society of Typographic Designers (*TypoGraphic*); London College of Communication (*Typos*), International Typeface Corporation, Ltd/fonts.com (*U&lc*); Dr Martin Mäntele (Head of Archive)/Hochschule für Gestaltung, Deutschland (*ulm*); Derek Brazell/AOI (*Varoom*); The MIT Press (*Visible Language*); Jaco Emmen (*de Vorm*); Stichting Industriële Vormgeving/Tel Design (*Vorm*); Freek Kroesbergen (*Vomberichten*); Studio Dumbar (*Zee Zucht*); Vladimir Krichevski, Yelena Chernevich (*Da!*).

Impact 2.0
—
**Design magazines, journals
and periodicals [1974–2016]**

Unit 28

Editors:
Tony Brook
Adrian Shaughnessy

Creative Director:
Tony Brook

Writer:
Adrian Shaughnessy

Sub-editor:
Susannah Worth

Design:
Tony Brook
Rachel Dalton
Jack Grafton
Andrea Guccini
Claudia Klat
Callin Mackintosh
Tommy Spitters

Researcher:
Alice Shaughnessy

Proof Reader:
Cathy Johns

Production Manager:
Sam Stevenson

Publishing Director:
Patricia Finegan

Typefaces:
Futura Maxi
Rotis Serif

Paper:
80gsm Multioffset
300gsm Starline creamback

Printer:
Die Keure

ISBN: 978-0-9932316-9-8

Unit Editions
Studio 2
33 Stannary Street
London SE11 4AA
United Kingdom
T +44 (0)20 7793 9555
F +44 (0)20 7793 9666
post@uniteditions.com
www.uniteditions.com

This and other Unit Editions
books can be ordered direct
from the publisher's website:

www.uniteditions.com